Queer musings of a One-Time Boy Skater

Joe Bainbridge

Queer Musings

of a One-Time

Boy Skater

by Joe Bainbridge

Queer Musings of a One-Time Boy Skater

ISBN: 9798835116676

IG: @jbainbr

"Our goal is to be that bridge

so that way if people want to try [figure skating] - but the parents

don't want to go full out right away - then we'll come step in, give

them the skates for a few months for free, and then if they like

them they can get them for a really good discount, and it kind of

sets them on their way from there."

Trennt Michaud on *ToePick Apparel*

25% OF ALL PROCEEDS

WILL BE DONATED TO TOEPICK APPAREL

TO SUPPORT FUTURE BOY SKATERS

Table of Contents

for my girls,

Tara and Sarah.

Introduction

As someone who lives with anxiety, I have a tendency to overthink just about everything. At any given moment, there are thousands of thoughts running through my head. I'm constantly reliving every interaction I've had throughout the day, no matter how small, while also revisiting some of my past trauma, just for kicks. And this, all while trying, and usually failing, to convince myself that not everybody hates me.

And here you thought *Jenga* was a balancing act.

On the best of days, I may experience less than ideal levels of productivity due to my intrusive and constantly racing thoughts. On the worst, I may stay awake the entire night just staring at the ceiling, thinking about whether a particular social interaction I had that day made me seem nice but needy or needy but nice. Believe me. There's a difference.

And believe me, through the COVID-19 pandemic, there were a lot of worst days.

So a few months ago, I started writing down my feelings and observations at the suggestion of my therapist at the time. She thought it might be a productive way to work through some of my recurring issues. Perhaps putting things down on paper would start to give my experiences closure, and help me to move on.

It was certainly worth a shot.

I never intended to write a book.

But as I continued to record my daily musings, I started to see two recurring motifs emerging in my writing: figure skating and queerness. Now, I suppose that this wasn't a particularly surprising revelation. I mean, I spent nearly ten years of my childhood into my adolescence as a competitive pair skater, and have been a queer man for thirty-two years and counting. Minus that one summer I developed a massive crush on Hilary Duff.

Oh wait. That was also gay. Nevermind.

But I realized that I have something important to say about the intersection between figure skating and queerness, and how they have both shaped my experiences to make me into the (highly anxious, but super loveable?) man I am today.

And the more I think about it, the more timely I think this discussion is right now. These days, it seems as if more and more first class athletes are comfortable enough to share their truths, even at the height of their careers. And I couldn't be happier.

Representation matters. And with positive queer role models like gay football player Carl Nassib and trans runner Nikki Hilts, both of whom came out in 2021, the once archaic world of professional sports seems to be bounding toward wokeness.

As a high school teacher, I'm more than thrilled that my students get to see these openly queer figures thriving, and finding support not only within their controlled sports communities, but almost universally. Growing up in the 90s, that level of visibility just wasn't a thing.

But what about the rest of us? The amateur athletes, and dedicated spectators, and lovers and dreamers and has-beens? The passionate plebeians, if you will. Where's our story? Where's our representation? We deserve visibility too.

And therein lies approximately ninety-five percent of the reason behind my decision to publish this never-intended-to-be-a-book book. To give a voice to a cross-section of the figure skating world that seems underrepresented. To share my stories with all of my friends and students, and future friends and future students. My stories as a one-time boy skater.

The other five percent is for the fame and fortune.

"My first pair [of figure skates] was actually white skates

because my family was [hesitant],

and where I was from, it was hard to get black skates anyway."

Trennt Michaud

Bibbidi-Bobbidi-Boo

Growing up, my family was never particularly well off. Now don't get me wrong, we always had food on the table and a roof over our heads, and my parents always did their best to keep us from feeling left out. But sometimes the more lavish things in life were just out of our reach. Like the latest *Archie Double Digest* at the grocery checkout and the good number two pencils.

But my mother always knew how to penny pinch with the best of them. Producers from TLC's *Extreme Couponing* would call our house day and night asking her for her thrifting expertise. Ok. That's a bit of an exaggeration, but it's closer to reality than you may think. Still, after a series of layoffs at my dad's work, and her own inability to find a job in her field, even my frugal as fuck mother was finding it difficult to stretch a dollar.

My dad works harder than anyone I know. After dropping out of high school before the eleventh grade to work in the local shipyard, he balanced full-time shift work with night classes to earn his diploma after my sister and I came along. His dedication to setting a strong example for my sister and I was truly inspiring.

My mother, on the other hand, left a senior administrative position at one of the largest plants in Sarnia's infamous chemical valley in order to raise us kids. And by the time we were both in school, her secretarial degree from the nearby community college was all but obsolete.

At this point in time, Windows 95 was steadily increasing in popularity, and computer operating systems were becoming the new norm. Even in Sarnia, a small city in Southern Ontario known for being nearly impenetrable to progress, every business within a hundred mile radius had made the shift to an automated bookkeeping system.

And despite taking night classes from the nearly prehistoric librarian at the local library to help prepare for this new digital age, my technology-challenged mother simply couldn't keep up.

To put things into perspective, my family didn't own a desktop computer until my final year of high school. Whenever we were asked to complete a research assignment for homework, I would dust off our highly outdated (in other words abhorrently racist) encyclopedias and pray to the gods above that I didn't make a fool of myself.

Unintentional bigotry was always just a paraphrase away.

I would then put on my best Virginia Woolf impression, minus the psychotic episodes of course, and sit down at the manual typewriter to begin work on my latest literary achievement, appropriately titled "My Third Grade Science Project."

To this day, my mother still occasionally asks me to "fax" my sister if she needs to ask her an important question.

Needless to say, there was no way in hell my mother was going to make it in the new world of computational contraptions and digital doodads. So my family had to make it work on a single not-always-reliable income. And for some time, it did work.

After all, like every good Boomer housewife, my mother was a master of planning a groovy shindig with nothing but some spare change and a prayer.

Many a night, my sister and I would both load into our big red wagon, and my mom would pull us ten blocks to the local library. No wonder her guns were bigger than Hulk Hogan's.

There, we would each select a movie, usually a *Faerie Tale Theatre* VHS for me and the latest Mary-Kate and Ashley *You're Invited* VHS for my sister, and before returning home, the three of us would buy as many penny candies from the 7-Eleven across the street as our handful of nickels could afford.

For a simple-minded six-year-old, it was a dream come true. But just as I was starting to become accustomed to our little corner of the world, I found my life's calling.

Despite our occasional feelings of loathing for choosing to live in a climate where the wind is so cold that it hurts your face, my family have been faithful fans of winter sports for as long as I can remember. As a former OHL superstar who "just missed the NHL draft of 1978," my father always insisted that we watch every disappointing Toronto Maple Leafs game as a family.

But blazing metosexual that he was (he always considered Cher to be his favourite musical artist and I would surely rank *Sex and the City* as must-see TV), my father didn't disciminate when it came to ice escapades, and we would watch figure skating and

22

speed skating with equal fervor. Especially during the Olympics. And it was while watching the 1998 Winter Games around our opulent 24-inch picture tube that my life was changed forever.

I remember the very instant that I first fell in love. We were all on the edge of our seats as a fifteen-year-old Tara Lipinski successfully completed the final jump of her flawless long program, throwing her arms up in the air in a moment of pure triumph. I can still remember the look on her face, and the magic of that moment. It felt like the entire world let out a collective cheer in honour of this unprecedented ingenue. And at that very moment, I decided that I would be next.

But when I told my parents of my new Olympic dreams, they were less than enthusiastic. At this point, I had already been taking CanStake lessons for over a year, to prepare to follow in my dad's footsteps as a nearly successful hockey star. In retrospect, my parents' reaction to my announcement that I wanted to be the next Tara Lipinski was more than commendable.

My mother had been a figure skater herself, well into her days at Lambton College. And from the ice carnivals of days gone by, she had the Dorothy Hamill-inspired glamour shots to prove it. Both she and my father were entirely supportive of my desire to commit to a passion that my toxicly masculine cousins would forever refer to as a "girl's sport." But the financial repercussions of the venture were not lost on them for a moment.

It should come as no surprise that figure skates aren't exactly a hot commodity for young boys, especially in my very close-minded town. And due to their mysterious and elusive nature, they cost upwards of an arm and a leg to purchase: an arm, a leg, two ears, and a middle finger, to be exact. And that's not even considering the cost of private lessons, competition fees, or occasional (but not too occasional) over-priced arena fries.

So in order to save money, my dad came up with the brilliant idea to purchase a suitable pair of offensively affordable women's figure skates and spray paint them black. And to the untrained eye, the deception was nearly flawless. But deep down, I knew the truth. And I felt like a complete fraud. Sure, the skates served their required purpose. But they didn't inspire any confidence in my abilities as a soon-to-be Olympic contender.

I've always been at the complete mercy of my emotions. I have a lot of feelings. And those feelings always make themselves known on my face, regardless of my desperate attempts to keep them hidden. So when I stepped on the ice for my first private lesson bearing an obvious stink eye, my coach knew something was up. And it wasn't long before she sniffed out the root cause of my obvious displeasure: my goddamn fraudulent footwear.

Now, Sarnia really is the kind of community where everyone is a friend-of-a-friend. And news certainly travels fast. I mean, everyone and their mother heard about that one time my cousin had explosive diarrhea in the middle of her dance recital. I still take offense that she thinks I was the one to start that heinous rumour (and I'm sincerely sorry for bringing it up again now).

My story made its way through the grapevine in record time. And when a local matriarch of a well-known family of generational figure skaters heard about my plight, she didn't hesitate to step in. She was my very own figure skating fairy godmother, if you will.

As the mother of two bold and boisterous boy skaters of

her own, Pat Jackson was as resolute as she was warm. She invited us into her home with open arms, and offered not only a highly-discounted pair of her youngest son's custom-made (read "diamond-encrusted") skates, but also insisted on putting together my first competition outfit. Think James Bond, but with exquisitely tacky gold sequins. Because drama.

As the only boy skater at the Moore Skating Club, I thought I was the only one of my kind. But meeting Don and Morgan in their home at my first fitting, I felt a strong sense of fraternity. It felt as if we were immediately bonded through our mutual and unconventional devotion.

And having my measurements taken fulfilled another lifelong dream. Even at the tender age of eight, I knew the value of custom couture. I was Claudia Schiffer being fitted for an exclusive Valentino gown. And it couldn't have felt more right.

Returning to the ice with my very own pair of authentic boys figure skates, and a darling costume to boot, gave me the confidence I needed to start my competitive figure skating career. And the road to the podium was clear, all thanks to the kindness and generosity of the Jacksons.

I often reflect on this opportunity I was given. I'm so very lucky to have found people in my corner to help me along the journey. And it continues to amaze me how familiar my story is within the skating community. Familiar enough to have inspired charitable initiatives like pair skater Trennt Michaud's *ToePick Apparel*, which itself provides affordable figure skates to young boys in need.

Figure skating changed my life. And while my Olympic pursuits never came to fruition, my lifelong love of the sport was more than worth the effort. And whether on or off the ice, I know that I will be a boy skater for as long as I live.

In My Skating Bag

★ Custom-made authentic boy's *figure skates* courtesy of your

   fairy godmother, Pat Jackson

★ Black *skate guards* that you will forget to remove before

   entering the ice more times than you'd like to admit,

   leading to at least two near-death experiences

★ Licensed Hercules *skate cozies* to remind you that if Herc

   can go from "Zero to Hero " in no time flat, then you can

   learn to land your damn axel clean

★ *Sony Discman* to listen to your competition music and get

   yourself into the zone

★ *Britney Spears CDs* that you actually listen to while you

   pretend to listen to your boring ass competition cuts

★ *Spare change*, preferably quarters, to buy as many delicious

   sour keys from the arena concessions as you can afford

★ *Sasha Cohen's "Fire On Ice"* to remind you of the beauty and

   excellence you strive for every single day

"I think masculinity is what you believe it to be.

To me, masculinity is all my perception.

I think masculinity and femininity is something that's

very old fashioned."

Johnny Weir

He's So Unusual

I knew I would have to get down to business if I was going to follow in Tara's footsteps. So between receiving her scores and the official medal ceremony, I had already started planning out my dream Olympic routine. I decided that a carefully-curated medley of Disney songs would be the most appropriate choice of music, featuring iconic moments from my favourite Disney princesses. After all, I was practically a shoo-in for Belle.

Without reliable access to an arena of our own, my sister and I had come up with a completely brilliant plan. By tying plastic grocery bags over our feet, we were able to minimize the friction between our tender tootsies and the orange shag carpet in our dingy basement, perfectly simulating a real ice rink. At least, that's what it felt like for two naive country bumpkins with overly active imaginations. And it was in this magical makeshift arena that I choreographed my first (and only as of this writing) competitive skating routine.

In my mind, it was a masterpiece. All fancy footwork and dramatic flourishes. And spirited spiral sequences and inflated *Ina Bauers*. And layback spins. Layback spins were without a doubt my favourite. Keep in mind that my earliest points of reference were Oksana Baiul and Kristi Yamaguchi. The routine certainly wasn't going to be understated.

But when I shared my vision with my skating coach, my little bubble burst. "That's not a boy's number."

She proceeded to explain that, as a young male skater, the judges would have certain expectations for my routine, from the music selection to the costuming to the choreography itself. For my music, I was given a choice between "Mission Impossible" and "James Bond." And the suggested costuming options were equally as uninspired (the aforementioned gold sequins were clearly at my own personal request).

I was shook. Here I wanted opulence, and instead I was being offered restrained. Nancy Kerrigan would never have stood for this treatment. Nevertheless, I bit my tongue. What else could I do? And I performed my plucky "Mission Impossible" number week after week, with as much feigned enthusiasm as I could muster. Which was probably not all that much. I mean, remember that stink eye? It was starting to become my signature look.

"Oh no, that's just his face."

However, I wasn't the only one sporting a contemptuous expression. Despite my dapper digs and laddish choreography, when the boys in my class caught wind of my extracurricular interests, the slander was swift and unwavering. Especially from the brutish hockey hopefuls (and former friends) I had shared the ice with over the years.

But even before my revelation during the 1998 Winter Olympics, I was starting to question whether or not playing hockey was for me. I just didn't see the appeal of chasing a puck back and forth for hours at a time. How very canine. Besides, there were no jumps in hockey. Why would I want to stay grounded when I could know what it feels like to fly?

In my mind, there was nothing emasculating about the sheer athleticism required to perform the diverse array of elements required of any competitive figure skating routine. So it never made sense to me why other boys my age would constantly refer to figure skating as a "girl's sport." In my personal experience with the sport, it did not embrace femininity in male skaters. Quite the opposite, in fact.

Some of the earliest feedback I received about my skating skills suggested that I needed to demonstrate more strength on the ice and less whimsy. In other words, I needed to skate more like a man. And even at such a young age, the irony of my situation was not lost on me.

While my peers harassed me relentlessly because of my competitive figure skating career, with "fairy" and "faggot" among the most frequent slights, at the same time, I seemed to be too feminine to have a proper place in the sport. And somehow, that hesitation towards less "macho" male skaters extended far beyond my regional bubble and into the world of Olympic-level athletics.

I remember watching Johnny Weir perform his infamous "The Swan" routine during the 2006 Olympic Games. Perfectly capturing the movement of a veteran ballet dancer, I was riveted by his beauty and grace on the ice. Upon his return in the following

Olympic cycle, Johnny pushed the boundaries of male skating one step further, incorporating traditionally female movement into his program, and donning a fabulous pink and black mesh corset with faux leather detail.

Now that was a costume worthy of even the most discerning of divas.

But when controversy arose surrounding some offensive remarks made by two French Canadian commentators, questioning Johnny's gender and his place in the men's event, I realized how little progress had been made in my more than a decade with the sport. And I took those remarks very personally.

I saw so much of myself in Johnny Weir. And as craven as it may be, I was grateful that by 2010, my days of competitive skating were long behind me. Following those remarks, I don't know how it would have felt, skating to centre ice, waiting for my program music to begin. Knowing that I might be judged not only on my skating skills, but also on my very identity.

Actually, I know exactly how it would have felt.

It would have felt rejective.

And intrusive.

And demeaning.

But yet another decade has passed since that controversy, and a move towards more inclusivity in the sport finally seems to be well on its way. And it's about damn time.

In honour of Pride month, Olympic hopefuls Jason Brown and Paul Poirier came out as gay. Vocal LGBT advocates Kaitlyn Weaver and Amber Glenn continue to bring visibility to a highly underserved group within the skating community. And the positive support for non-binary pair skater Timothy LeDuc during the 2022 Olympic season is a notable sign of progress. Especially for the typically impartial ISU.

And rather than the rigid duality between male and female technique, skaters are coming to be recognized more and more for their versatility. US Champion Bradie Tennell offsets elegant spiral sequences with tenacious, high-energy programs and a strapping jumping technique. In a statement-making black pantsuit, no less. And she is applauded for it. World Bronze Medalists Paul Poirier and Piper Gilles rock the ice in flamboyant Elton John-inspired costumes, all but eliminating the often inflexible gender roles associated with ice dancing. And their rhythm dance scores among the best in the world.

I often wonder whether the gendered binary of male versus female athletes will ever become a relic in itself. But at the very least, I hope that someday we'll see more diversity within the pairs event. Women skating with women and men skating with men. And non-binary individuals skating with men. And women skating with non-binary individuals. People skating with people. Period.

Now wouldn't that be something.

"Male figure skating is different than female figure skating: we're not America's sweetheart."

Scott Hamilton

I Want Candy

I definitely inherited my sweet tooth from my mother's side, especially my Grandma O'Neill. Although, in this case the word "tooth" is a bit of a misnomer. Marjorie lost her own pearly whites as a young woman, and she wore a pair of fierce, oversized dentures for as long as I can remember. Think Jiggly Caliente circa *RuPaul's Drag Race: All Stars*. Post-veneers, of course.

Those resin chiclets were a major source of trauma for me growing up. You know that awful recurring nightmare where you lose all of your teeth, one-by-one, and wake up feeling like you've been punched in the gut by John Cena? Well, that nightmare isn't too far from reality for most middle-aged descendents of Queen Maeve. The "luck of the Irish" certainly does not refer to our soft, easily-stained teeth.

Of course, it didn't help that at some point during every trip to the dentist, Doctor Doherty would encourage me to take extra care with my oral hygiene. "After all, you have your grandmother's teeth."

Shudder.

What a handsome inheritance. It's no wonder my teenage and early adult years were spent overbrushing away nearly all of my natural enamel. Go big or go home, right?

But back to Marge, or as my grandpa always called her, "Old Jore." Her motto was quite simple: "What's the point of dinner without dessert?" And so far as I can remember, she lived by that motto faithfully. In fact, the only thing sweeter than Marjorie's diet was her saccharine disposition.

Despite living with diabetes for her entire adult life, without fail, Grandma O'Neill always had a sweet treat nearby, whether a dusty stick of sugar-free gum from the bottom of her purse or a room-temperature can of Diet Coke from her oversized (and perpetually ice-less) plastic cooler. And her hoarder-adjacent home was consistently stacked with more sugary sweets than the novelty Candy Shoppes you find in cozy Ontario tourist towns. You know, those towns where they film only the cheesiest of *Lifetime Network* films?

Side note. From one sugar-lover to another, you must never under any circumstances buy candy from those tacky, faux-vintage shops. You're almost certain to pay a hefty premium, if only for that additional "P" and entirely indulgent "E." Kings and queens of *Candyland,* hooked on phonics we are not. We just want our quick saccharine fix.

Besides, the rush is always free-of-charge at grandma's house. Over the years, every time my family visited their farm, my sister and I would over-indulge in so many Cosmic Brownies and Oatmeal Creme Pies that it would surprise me if *Little Debbie* didn't suffer a major financial loss when grams left us for the good place.

And I don't mean "the good place" that's actually "the bad place," like in that much too self-aware Kristen Bell sitcom. Oh, snicklefritz. Sorry. I suppose it's too late for a spoiler alert now. But honestly, if anyone deserves luxury in the afterlife, it is without a doubt Marjorie O'Neill.

This is the woman who volunteered to chauffeur feeble seniors from the local retirement home to the Victoria Playhouse, the nearby professional theatre, never seeming to realize that she was often older than the elders in her care. This is the woman who sent a card to each of my highschool friends on their birthday, even when I forgot. Your guess is as good as mine as to how she knew each date of birth in the first place. Friends in high places, I guess? Like Santa Claus. Or Jack Bauer.

This is the woman who continued to buy Christmas gifts for each of my uncle's vast convoy of ex-girlfriends long after they had broken up, just to make sure that they still felt like a part of the family. It was a sentiment in stark contrast to the sincere "beat it bitch" mentality I shared with my mother towards each of his self-absorbed conquests.

But Marjorie O'Neill was truly an angel among us. And while her influence on my eating habits is sure to lead me to an early grave, it also qualifies me as a notable expert in the study of sweets. It was under Marjorie's careful guidance that I earned my masters degree in confectionary science. With distinction. Through years of extensive quantitative experimentation and careful research development (translation: emotional eating and bonbon benders), I have ultimately discovered that there are four marketplace candies objectively better than the rest.

And what better way is there to honour the woman who supported me more than anyone else in the world than by sharing my secrets to superior succulence.

Feel free to take notes. I'll speak slowly:

In fourth place we have Tropical Skittles. From pineapple to passionfruit, this assortment of vacation-centric flavours is the elite choice within the Skittles brand. And despite steadily rising grocery prices, they're still slightly more affordable than a honeymoon in Hawaii. Very slightly.

In third place are Licorice Allsorts. With a variety of candy-coated textures, held together with the chewy adhesive of tangy black licorice, it should come as no surprise that wise elders across the globe tried to keep this scrumptious secret from younger generations. We shall not be fooled.

The runner-up is Reese's Peanut Butter Cups. Much like pineapple on pizza, the combination of salty and sweet has forever been a divisive topic among top culinary experts. But considering the unrivaled complexity and versatility of this arachidous treat, the right side of history should be readily apparent.

But the hands-down winner is Wine Gums. Nothing feels more grown-up than enjoying a glass or two of fine red wine in your smoking room after a hard day at the office, but pilfering these fruit-flavoured candies from the pocket of my dad's favourite leather jacket as a young lad certainly came close. These champagne gummies are the taste of nostalgia.

And there you have it, folks. No, sorry. I won't be taking any questions at this time. These rankings are not up for debate. However, there were a few runners-up worth noting:

HONOURABLE MENTIONS:

First, the highly underrated mid-tempo pop classic "Candy" by prolific singer-songwriter Mandy Moore. Sigh. Late 90s Mandy. We just didn't deserve you.

Former Canadian pairs skater Candace "Candy" Jones, perhaps best known for her no-hands "death spiral." Feel free to look it up. But to be completely honest, it's not as cool as it sounds. Like, it should probably be called a "reckless abandonment" spiral.

The stunning candy couture made by Roxxy Andrews from the fifth season of *RuPaul's Drag Race*. Admittedly, Roxie Andrews is far from my favourite queen. But she made a gorgeous floor-length gown entirely out of rainbow licorice strings. Props.

And who could forget the ever-ratched, not so sweet Kandy Muse. Her top-three placement in season thirteen is still one of the greatest unsolved mysteries of the world.

Ok, ok. I know it's a bit of a stretch. But did you really expect me to get off on talking about candy without making reference to divalicious drag queens and bubblegum pop? What kind of a tired-ass showgirl do you take me for?

Besides, I feel like Marjorie would have liked that RuPaul and her Drag Race. At the very least, she would have appreciated the lavish costumes and lively lip syncs. And perhaps she would have felt some sense of kinship towards an entire demographic of women who wear just as much lipstick as she did. Of course, most of her own bright red liner ended up on those darned dentures, but that's beside the point.

I never had a chance to come out to my Grandma O'Neill, but that doesn't bother me so much anymore. I know she would have approached my queerness the same way she approached every other aspect of her too-short life: with grace and gratitude.

And so much love.

"I always felt like I was so big and

[my legs] made me look stocky and I didn't like them.

And then it took me a long time to realize all the things that they

do for me— all the times that they took me through my programs,

through training, through running — and they're actually

incredible."

Gracie Gold

Body Love

We didn't have a Starbucks in Sarnia until 2010, a fact that my city-bred uncle never missed an opportunity to complain about whenever he visited during the holidays. "Man cannot live on Tim Hortons alone." Nevertheless, despite the empirically-proven correlation between overpriced beans and athletic ability (Seriously. Have you ever seen Olympic gold-medalist Jamie Sale without a cuppa joe in hand?), Lambton County seemed to be a hotspot for elite-level male figure skaters.

Maybe it was some strange and fortunately favourable undetected contagion wafting from the stacks of Sarnia's famed Chemical Valley. Or perhaps in an area with one of the most senile populations in the province, the sheer number of lascivious old bitties still wildly enamored with ladies-man Elvis Stojko created a Boomer-driven boom in the sport, scheming seniors far and wide, shepherding their grandsons to follow in his virile footsteps.

What nostalgic nanna wouldn't want to see their little

pride-and-joy hustle through a cheeky Stolko-inspired skating routine clad entirely in black pleather?

Whatever the reason, Lambton County has produced some of the most talented and enduring skaters in the sport. Of course, three-time Canadian pairs national champion Michael Marinaro immediately comes to mind, but also junior nationals pair skater Don Jackson (oh yes, the very same one who sold me my first ever pair of boys figure skates) and even *Disney on Ice* artistic director and choreographer Adam Loosely.

I consider myself incredibly lucky to have skated alongside such incredible role models and peers. What's that oh-so-prophetic cliché? If you want to be great, surround yourself with greatness. But their continuous success also gave me so many expectations to live up to. Throughout my formative years, I couldn't help but compare myself with these exceptional men, especially in terms of the way I looked.

Believe it or not, despite my towering stature and broad football shoulders (inherited directly from my mother), I was a rather small child. Having been born a full four weeks premature, it took me several years to catch up to my peers. Now my sister, on the other hand, was a real chubster. Coincidentally, we actually shared the same due date, exactly three years apart: February 28th. But being born almost a week late, she made her entrance into the world as a roly-poly bundle of chunk. Talk about backrolls.

Alyssa Edwards had nothing on her.

But by the time I started skating competitively, I had not only caught up to the other boys my age, but surpassed them in terms of both height and weight.

I blame it on my all too frequent indulgence in sweets (Damn you, Marjorie), especially wine gums and licorice allsorts. Oh yes. Even at the prime age of twelve, these old-man candies were my favourite treats. If you aren't at least somewhat convinced that I'm actually a ninety year-old man catfishing as a millennial, have you really been reading that closely?

But back to body image. Realistically, my physique actually had more to do with my natural body frame than with my eating or exercise habits. Nevertheless, it didn't take long for me to realize that I didn't look like the other competitors.

While the other boy skaters were sinewy and angular, I was husky and round-faced. And it certainly didn't help that my seventh-grade gym teacher constantly reminded me of her greatly tempered expectations for me, considering that my body was "less athletic" than the other boys in my class.

I had skated against Michael Marinaro a couple of years prior on the singles circuit, and at the time, we seemed to be well-matched in terms of skill. But at more recent outings, I couldn't help but notice that he had begun skating in later and later flights. In a short period of time, Michael had made leaps and bounds in his ability, while I had only marginally improved.

One day, while practicing my axel (a jump also known as the very bane of my pre-teen existence), I became so frustrated that I gave up and sat down at middle ice. "I'm just not built for this." While the melting ice soaked through my Adidas joggers, I tearfully explained to my coach my observations about how being "out of shape" limited me from advancing in the sport.

But Deb wasn't having any of it. That day, my coach taught me a very important lesson. Being healthy does not always mean being thin, just as being thin does not alway mean being healthy.

And just because I was sturdy and full-bodied didn't mean I was

incapable or out of shape.

Of course, Deb's lesson wasn't merely rhetorical. And even

though her coaching style was certainly more Gordon Bombay

than Abby Lee Miller, it was still her job to help me to achieve

certain physical goals. And despite being out-of-breath after

performing my competition routine three times in a row, I had to

agree that my stamina wasn't the issue.

My momentary desire for Deb to choke on her coffee has

faded considerably ("Three times in a row? Full-out? Seriously?"),

but her lesson about appreciating my body has carried with me into

adulthood. And as a young gay man navigating a community

notorious for its tunnel-vision focus on physical attractiveness, that

lesson has been absolutely invaluable.

I was a very late bloomer. Minus a stage kiss in a local

theatre production of *RENT*, *Never Been Kissed* would have been a

perfectly appropriate title for my university days. I mean, I didn't

even start dating until I was twenty-five. And in gay years, that's practically middle-aged. I guess you can call me *The 40-Year-Old Virgin.* Minus (most of) the back hair.

But despite my delayed start, after diving headfirst into the glamorous worlds of Grindr and Growlr and Scruff (oh my) it didn't take long for me to find my first boyfriend.

Colin was a beautiful, gym-obsessed ginger with a green-thumb and a taste for gourmet cooking. And he had a massive snake. Literally. Her name was Sophie, and she was a seven-foot boa constrictor. She lived in a (probably safe) glass enclosure at the end of his bed.

Red flag?

I mean, no more than the fact that he still lived with his ex.

Red. Flag.

I was still a virgin when I met Colin, and we dated for almost three months before we slept together. Now, keep in mind that my predominant references for romance were cheesy rom coms from the 90s, like *She's All That* and *My Best Friend's Wedding.* And just like my girls Julia, Rachel, and Drew, I wanted to be in love for my first time.

One night, after dropping his ex off for a sleazy late-night booty call, and arriving home more than slightly tipsy after a trashy stag-and-doe, I finally told Colin that I loved him and that I was ready. So we both stumbled to his third-floor bedroom, got out the "slip-and-slide" (condoms and lube), and did the deed. How romantic. You must have missed that scene from *Casablanca*.

But the next time I saw Colin, he dumped me.

Impeccable timing, right?

I was devastated. And to be completely honest, I still deal with the consequences of that trauma. According to my therapist, I subconsciously connect intimacy with abandonment. Talk about more fun than a barrel of monkeys. After years of unpacking the situation in therapy, I understand that there were countless reasons that our relationship had a definite expiration date. But at the time, I could only think of one.

I was too fat.

I admit my flawed reasoning was likely a result of my very limited understanding of gay culture. My habitual midnight viewing of *Queer as Folk* while my parents were asleep wasn't exactly an encouraging representation. Four fit and fabulous white men raving their way through the seedy underground club culture of Pittsburgh, Pennsylvania? Talk about relatable.

Nevertheless, all of the conversations I had with Colin about working out and going to the gym replayed in my head. And I started to rewrite his personal body issues as criticisms about my own appearance. I convinced myself that in order to win him back, all I would need to do was sculpt my body to the perfection of Brad Pitt in *Thelma and Louise.*

If you haven't witnessed that particular moment of cinematic excellence, for shame. A plague on both your houses. But to appease my Gen Z readers (and all of the dirty old twink chasers out there), Tom Holland in *Spider-man: Homecoming* is an equivalent comparison.

In any case, it would be a piece of cake. Except no cake. Stay away from cake. Don't even think about cake.

I started running every evening, usually for a couple of hours at a time. And within a few weeks, I saw noticeable results. The metabolism of twenty-five year-old men is pure wizardry. But still, the transformation was too gradual. I needed to reach peak Adonis status before Colin forgot about me and moved on to his next conquest.

So I made some minor dietary changes to expedite my pursuit of the perfect body. In other words, I subsisted for almost an entire month on only bananas and oatmeal. And in no time, the compliments started rolling in. My girlfriends at work just couldn't stop complaining about the injustice of it all. "It's just so much easier for men to lose weight." Little did they know that I was consuming less than five-hundred calories a day, and getting weaker by the minute.

A single picture exists of me at my most lean. And it stirs within me such a strange mix of emotions. On one hand, I look hot as fuck. There's a reason why it was my *Grindr* profile for years to come. I mean, even I would do me. But on the other hand, it brings me back to a time when I felt my absolute lowest.

That photo reminds me of rock bottom.

I dropped almost forty pounds in just a little over a month. And as my weight disappeared, so did my endurance. My nightly runs were becoming shorter and shorter. At one point, I could barely make it through three repeats of Carly Rae Jepsen's "Tonight I'm Getting Over You" (hands down the best break-up song in the known and unexplored universe) before falling to the ground in complete exhaustion.

And one night, while I was sitting there in the grass, struggling to catch my breath, the voice of an old friend popped into my head. "In the moonlight, don't you think about him. Sister, you're much better off without him." Actually, that was two-time Tony Award-winner Sutton Foster. Great advice, but not the diva of the hour in this particular situation.

It was the voice of my former coach, Deb Dauw, that visited me in my moment of crisis: "Being thin does not always mean being healthy."

I stopped to check myself and came to a not-so-startling conclusion. I was definitely not healthy. I could barely make it to the end of the block without feeling dizzy, let alone complete my *Mission Impossible* routine from almost fifteen years prior three times in a row. And I made the necessary adjustments to get my life, and my health, back on track.

In all honesty, my relationship with my self-image hasn't always been perfect, but I do believe that figure skating helped me to appreciate my body for what it can do, rather than for what it looks like. And that lesson has served me very well through my experiences with the sometimes overly cruel world of trying to find love as a gay man.

No fats or femmes? No problem.

Your loss, headless torso. Your loss.

"When I was young and at training,

there were times when I would go to school [and]

there'd be classmates that bullied me for skating.

I was being made fun of for doing what I loved to do,

so I just let my love for skating supersede any of that negativity."

Adam Rippon

Universal Truths

All self-identifying "rink rats" should come to understanding the following list of universal truths:

1. Regardless of your sex, skate size, or political affiliation, a delicate T-stop at centre ice is sure to make you feel like the queen mother herself.

2. If you are the only boy skater at your club, you are considered to be a novelty, and will be required to perform a cheeky boys number at every fall, winter, and spring showcase.

   Music suggestions include but are not limited to "Macho, Macho Man," selections from the Beach Boys, "Wild, Wild West," or the theme from the latest James Bond film.

3. The canned strawberry Fruitopia from the arena vending machine always tastes better than the flavourless jug you can buy at the store.

4. Although hockey ass gets all the attention, boy skater bum is the true MVP.

    I enter into evidence the posteriors of Paul Porier and Adam Rippon.

5. If you haven't spent part of your valuable ice time in the bathroom hiding from a group of bigoted townies, you aren't doing it right.

The Boys are Back in Town

I had only been skating for five years when my coach decided to leave her part-time gig at the Moore Skating Club to focus on her responsibilities as the new head coach in her hometown of Wallaceburg, Ontario. Haven't heard of Wallaceburg? Well, you're certainly not alone. It's a rather small community in Chatham-Kent, just off the picturesque (although highly polluted) St. Clair River. Google the "glass town of Canada" for reference.

Seriously? Glass town?

Who even comes up with this baloney?

Inching toward retirement, the drive back and forth from Wallaceburg to Mooretown was getting to be too much effort for Deb, especially during the long winter months. Keep in mind, this was in 2002, prior to the most acute impacts of climate change, when Canadian winters were still a force to be reckoned with. And Bratz dolls were all the rage.

What a time to be alive.

But before Deb left for good, she secretly asked me to come with her. How very unseemly. My very own recruitment scandal? I was shocked and appalled. And obviously, I was totally on board. At the time, I felt like Justin Timberlake, leaving the band to break out on my own. Cry me a river, Mooretown. I'm off to the big leagues (in comparison, anyway). Looking back, however, I think it was more akin to the plot of *The Fresh Prince of Bel-Air.*

During my last year at the Moore Skating Club, the bullying I was experiencing at school was worse than ever. And things were starting to get physical. I had my first full-fledged fistfight when a boy from my class referred to me as a "fucking faggot" after seeing me practicing at the arena. So I dug right down to the bottom of my soul and asked myself "What would Rocky Balboa do?"

And then I socked him one right in the sniffer.

If there's one thing my dad taught me, it's that Cher is the grand supreme of pop divas. Well, that and how to throw a punch.

Now for all of my students reading this, remember that violence is never the answer. Use your words instead. Take deep breaths, and practice appropriate conflict resolution.

Yada yada.

But in the moment, it worked like a charm. I had finally had enough, and I stood up for myself for the very first time. Jason immediately backed off, and it felt great. At least until the nearby supervision monitor, who just happened to catch the tail end of the altercation (of course), escorted me straight to the office. I was sent home for the rest of the day. And my mom got scared.

Ah, yes. There's that *Fresh Prince* reference coming back full-circle. It all makes perfect sense to me now, why my parents never batted an eye at having to drive over an hour, literally straight past the Moore Sports Complex, in hell or high water (one of my dad's favourite sayings) to the Wallaceburg Arena. They saw how much I was struggling at school and they wanted to protect me. And on some level, I know that I saw the same opportunity for a fresh start.

I stopped talking about figure skating at school, and before long, people started to assume that my days of deviance were behind me. It seemed like my peers had forgotten all about my highly contested passtime. And although it often felt as if I was living a double life (a triple life if you count the whole gay thing), things started to get better. There was just one thing that my parents and I hadn't accounted for in our scheme.

Travel hockey.

I was just in the midst of practicing my European Waltz, when out of the corner of my eye, I saw my mother racing from the bleachers towards the penalty box. Now, my mother is not exactly known for her speed. She's a textbook saunterer. So seeing her moving so frantically was more than enough to set me on edge. I hurried over to the boards to meet her.

In terms of her snooping skills, my mom would give Rita Skeeter a run for her money. And while grabbing her afternoon coffee from the arena concessions, she overheard the other moms talking about the hockey game later that day. They were all abuzz that the Wallaceburg Lakers had finally made it to the semi-finals after years of unremitting defeat. Of course, they would be playing none other than the reigning champs: the Mooretown Flags.

Fuck me gently with a chainsaw.

If someone from my school were to see me in my figure

skates, I knew that my torment would start anew. So I flew off the ice and headed toward the changerooms just as fast as my already shaking legs would take me. But just as I was about to turn the corner down the hallway, I saw an intimidating squadron of Mooretown Flags players quickly approaching from the other side of the double doors.

Led by none other than Nevio Paganelli. And in case you were wondering, yes, that is a totally made-up name. The real one sounded even more like your nonna's favourite pasta.

A heavyset Italian boy with a dirty stache and an impressive beer gut (especially for a thirteen-year-old), Nevio was basically the mafia king of my eighth grade class. And I was already on his radar. He and his cronies had humiliated me during gym class just a few weeks prior due to my less than impressive dodgeball skills.

"You throw like a pansy, Bainbridge."

If he saw me, he was sure to make the rest of my days at St. Joseph's Catholic School into a living hell.

Oh, did I forget to mention that I attended a Catholic elementary school? Silly me. I thought it would be immediately apparent from the freshly pressed choir robes hanging in my closet. Or at least from my mere speck of self-worth and deep-rooted feelings of shame.

Ba dum tsh.

You gotta laugh to keep from crying, right?

But I certainly wasn't laughing when Nevio and his army of pricks burst through the arena doors. Knowing that I would never make it to the dressing room without being detected, I made a split-second decision to duck into the bathroom to my left. I quickly locked myself in an open stall and drew my knees up to my chest so no one would see my blades under the door.

And I waited.

Nearly a half-hour later, I finally heard the combined sounds of skate blades scraping against the ice and unintelligible grunting that marks the beginning of every pregame hockey warmup. So I slipped my skates off and hid them under my sweater, then dashed outside in my stockinged feet and dove into our 1989 Volvo.

We drove home in near silence.

And that night, I cried myself to sleep.

Life at school certainly hadn't been perfect, but it had at least been tolerable. And to think that all of that could be lost in an instant was terrifying. Figure skating was dangerous. I was playing with fire. And I came to realize that sooner or later, I was almost certain to get burned.

That was the first time I seriously considered walking away from figure skating altogether. And to this day, I can't reconcile that feeling. The power that bullies have to take something that you love more than anything else in the world and make it into something vile and shameful is one of the truest forms of evil.

Ultimately, I was one of the lucky ones. My love for skating was enough to carry me through the remainder of the season. And by the time I started high school in the "big city" of Sarnia the following September, I found a strong group of like-minded individuals to support me and to shield me from the doubters and naysayers. And from Nevio Paganelli.

Although, there were some lasting effects of my experiences with bullying that I carried with me into adulthood, most notably my extreme mistrust of men. It would be years before I let down my guard enough to build meaningful friendships with "straight guys." And since then, I've learned a simple but universal truth.

Hetero men are boring.

I'm kidding. Mostly.

But how many lengthy conversations about *Call Of Duty* can you endure before you want to dig your brain out with a spoon? Through careful experimentation, I've found that my own limit falls somewhere between zero and one (but closer to zero, if I'm being completely honest).

Seriously, though. Everyone should be able to do what they enjoy. Openly and safe from ridicule. Period. That is the dream.

And perhaps we are starting to turn over a new leaf. I mean, at this point in my life, my days as a figure skater almost seem to be a novelty, and my icy anecdotes are generally accepted with curiosity and wonder rather than with scorn. Even in my classes, my students seem to be celebrated for their unorthodox avocations. It seems that artisans and philosophers are the new quarterbacks. But there is still progress to be made.

And I can't help but wonder. How many boy skaters won't survive the fight? How many champions-in-the-making will be forced to forfeit their dreams to avoid the ridicule of their peers, all before realizing their gold medal moment?

I guess we'll never really know.

"I think at a low level, and this is especially true when we think

about young children that are getting into sports for the first time,

we really need to stray away from this narrative that

certain sports are for boys and certain sports are for girls."

Paul Poirier

It's My Party

Regardless of the situation, my natural response to virtually every strong emotion is to cry. I'm sure it can be rather confusing for anyone unfortunate enough to witness the phenomena. Nevertheless, it seems to be entirely out of my control.

I cried tears of sadness at the end of Rupert Goold's *Judy*, suddenly realizing that I would never get to see my idol perform live. Nevermind the fact that Judy Garland had passed away over fifty years prior. The reminder was not appreciated.

I cried tears of fear when my grandmother insisted that *The Exorcist* is "what happens to little boys and girls who don't let Jesus into their hearts." If the movie itself wasn't scarring enough, her words certainly put the nail in the coffin. I mean, I was only seven at the time. One of the blessings and curses of having mostly older cousins is being regularly exposed to age-inappropriate content.

I cried tears of joy after unknowingly purchasing opening night tickets to the 2022 Broadway revival of *Into the Woods* starring

Patina Miller and Gavin Creel. And Sara freaking Bareilles. Of course, it wasn't long until my anxiety over what to wear kicked in. In the presence of Patti and Bernie, grandeur would be expected.

And on my drive home from school on an unremarkable Friday afternoon, I cried tears of … nothing? I'm actually not sure what I was feeling that day. Just that I was feeling.

But I definitely didn't inherit my overactive tear ducts from my dad. In my thirty-two years on this godforsaken planet, I've only seen him cry once, at the hospital, only moments after hearing my grandfather take his final strained breath.

After suffering a brain aneurysm almost five years prior, my grandmother had devoted herself to nursing him back to health. But after a recovery fraught with numerous setbacks and chronic dysphasia, after his most recent stroke, Ron deteriorated quickly throughout the night.

Even after watching his own father fade before his very eyes, my dad struggled to own up to his feelings. He quietly slipped away to cry in solitude in his Dodge Ram, leaving me sniveling unabashedly in the deserted hospital corridor.

I know that he wanted to stay strong for my grandmother. And his skewed Boomer impression of what it means to be a man didn't help. But for the most part, I think he just wanted to make his late father proud.

How ironic, considering it was actually my grandfather who first taught me that it's alright for boys to cry.

My sister was still in kindergarten when my grandpa moved in with our family. My grandmother had agreed to spend the better part of a year at an army base in Petawawa, helping her militant daughter to raise a young son. Worried about leaving her husband unattended for so long, she insisted that my grandfather move in with his eldest son.

Maybe her request was driven by a fear for his well-being. Or perhaps it was based on a sneaking suspicion that he might do something crazy and impulsive, like trading in the family vehicle for a sexy white Pontiac Firebird.

Yeah. That still happened.

In any case, Ron wasted no time in becoming a valuable member of the family. He started to petition for the grandfather-of-the-year award almost immediately, making regular appearances at our weekly skating practices and school assemblies.

But my grandpa's very favourite thing to do during his time living with our family was to listen to me and my sister practicing for our piano lessons.

From rock-and-roll to showtunes to jazz, Ron had always been a music fanatic. I mean, he owned at least three-quarters of Nana Mouskari's catalogue of 200 plus albums. But don't let that single blemish sway you from his otherwise impeccable taste. It was my grandfather who introduced me to Roberta Flack and Tom Jones and Frank Sinatra. And even the bewitching Peggy Lee.

So for our year-end recital, Sarah and I learned a beautiful duet arrangement of Alan Menken's and the late Howard Ashman's "Beauty and the Beast."

Beauty and the Beast was my favourite movie at the time. To be honest, it still is. And stockholm-syndrome aside, because of my grandfather, it likely will be for the rest of my life.

After practicing in secret for weeks, we decided to debut our new song for him. And while our performance at the recital would be instrumental only, we decided to sing along for our exclusive living room performance.

Ron was overcome with pride, in awe of the beautiful music my sister and I made together, and we barely made it to the end of the first verse before he started to cry.

Despite his intimidating physical stature and an occasional tendency to growl, there was nothing in the world that Ron loved more than being a grandpa. He was the definition of "gentle giant." A not-so-secret sensitive soul.

And I miss him dearly.

"If you have a bad day, it's just a bad day.

It's not your life. It's not everything.

And, you know, what goes up will come down

and it's just how life goes."

Sasha Cohen

Skating Elements

Highlights from a Regionals Debut

Throw Double Salchow

BV: 2.50   GOE: +0.50

A very good start. Things are looking promising at this point.

Side-By-Side Axels

BV: 1.10   GOE: -0.50

What guttersnipe decided on that extra half-rotation in the first place?

I think I may have injured my shoulder in the attempt.

Overhead Lift

BV: 2.30   GOE:-2.30

Aborted. The shoulder is definitely injured.

Side-by-Side Double Toe Loops

BV: 1.30   GOE: +0.25

This went surprisingly well, despite the axel blunders.

Maybe things are looking up?

Backward Inside Death Spiral

BV: 3.50   GOE: -1.50

Apparently the judges prefer it if your partner doesn't topple on top of you on the exit. Who knew?

End Scene

"I'm competitive. There's really no way around that.

I like to succeed and I like to figure things out.

I find that when you do — even if it's not always a success —

the process of getting there is exciting

and you never know what's going to happen."

Tara Lipinski

Anything You Can Do (I Can Do Better)

I've never considered myself to be a very competitive person, although my husband would care to disagree. In fact, he probably laughed out loud the first time he read this line. Actually, he might still be rolling on the floor as we speak. I should probably go check on him.

But to be completely honest, I don't foster the steadfast desire to win that I assume lives within all elite athletes. I mean, you don't get to be Kristi Yamaguchi without a ruthless hunger to be on top. What I do have is a very strong desire to live up to people's expectations, and major anxiety about letting the people that I care about down. And if that means I fight tooth and nail to make sure my fellow *Codenames* comrades are victorious, so be it.

After a few months, I was beginning to adjust to my new routine at the Wallaceburg Skating Club. And apart from escaping the rampant insults of my most malicious critics, changing clubs did have another notable perk. Her name was Alexa.

Alexa was a saucy and self-assured skating diva, and she owned the rink every time she hit the ice. It took all but five minutes for her to start chirping at me for skating too slowly, traveling on my spins, and constantly getting in her way. She drove me absolutely crazy. And she was my very best friend. I guess I'm just a glutton for punishment.

It wasn't long before we became inseparable. In fact, we hit it off so well that our coach suggested we team up and give pair skating the old college try.

So we did. And I loved it.

I knew after our very first practice that I had found my niche. Learning about throws and lifts and death spirals helped to reinvigorate my love of the sport, and shattered any thoughts I had about walking away. Mostly because I knew Alexa would break my kneecaps if I so much as tried.

Being part of a duo also helped me to conquer some of my performance anxiety. I never enjoyed being the centre of attention. I always let the pressure get to me. But sharing the spotlight with my very best friend was something I could really get behind.

I felt so empowered by our partnership.

But after our first competitive season as a pair, and an altogether disappointing debut at the regional championships, Alexa decided it was time for a change. It just so happened that the skating club just one small town over had an elite training program for more "serious" skaters. And in spite of our occasional tendency to sneak off in the middle of our lessons to binge eat sour keys from the arena concessions, we were nothing if not serious.

The only problem was the "serious" price tag attached. If custom boy figure skates were worth an arm and a leg, then private lessons at the Chatham Skating Club were sure to set you back at least a few NFL linebackers. Of course, with the amount we would save in secret sour keys, perhaps it would have evened out.

But that's one sacrifice we weren't willing to make.

So in the end, I just couldn't swing it, and we decided to cut back our pairs practices to two nights a week, and train solo every Wednesday afternoon. Although I missed my partner-in-crime during our midweek ice time, the agreed-upon legal separation provided us with the time we needed to reflect and to renew our commitment to one another.

Oh, who am I kidding? It's not like we were getting a divorce. At least not yet. And the benefits of our time apart were pretty simple: she had more time to work on her somewhat shameful spins while I could focus on my notably finite flexibility.

But the one skill we both had yet to master was landing a clean, fully-rotated axel. And we both decided that the best way to make that happen was to take turns attempting the jump for one another, and providing each other with (mostly) constructive feedback in the hopes of soon checking off our only remaining essential pre-novice element.

Let me tell you, in the grand tradition of *Paris is Burning*, some days the library was open. And, with each other's support, we both slowly but surely crept towards mastering the jump. Until the Judas turned against me, that is, and committed a most heinous and unforgivable sin.

On that fateful Friday evening, I knew something was off the instant Alexa stepped on the ice. Rather than starting with our traditional handheld tour around the rink, she slapped her guards down onto the boards and immediately beelined it for our coach. The tension built as she whispered into her ear, and Deb beckoned me over to join their conspiratorial tryst.

"Alexa has something she'd like to show you."

Deb encouraged her with a gentle nudge on her shoulder, and with a look of utter shame strewn across her face, Alexa skated off and proceeded to set up and land the most perfect axel known to man. It was truly transformative. The Meryl Streep of axels. Surely it deserved an Academy Award. Or three.

"I've been practicing with my Chatham friends," Alexa confessed. I know I should have been happy for her. Finally mastering a new skill is such an incredible accomplishment. And I wanted to be a good friend. But in that moment, my anxiety took the wheel, and my life flashed before my eyes.

Maybe that divorce wasn't such a stretch after all. Could I really be the man that she needed? Surely this new jumping sensation wouldn't let the likes of me hold her back. How long would it be before she decided to move on and start canoodling with those red-blooded Chatham boys? Would she be auditioning new skating partners before the week's end?

But as my mind carefully picked over every possible worst-case scenario in painstaking detail, my mouth made the greatest betrayal of them all. In what seemed like slow-motion, and in a near out-of-body experience, I heard myself say, "I learned how to land my axel this week too."

Oh fudge.

Now, under normal circumstances, I am honest to a fault, and my reputation precedes me. So with a twinkle in her eye, our coach immediately took my proclamation at face value. "That's wonderful news." I began to exhale a sigh of relief, and prepared to glide away to begin my warmup. But I wasn't going to get off that easy. "Why don't you show us?"

Double fudge.

Although it had been getting closer and closer to the ideal, my axel was still consistently under-rotated. But admitting that would be letting down both my coach and my skating partner. And that certainly wouldn't do. So I prayed to the only deity that I knew I could depend on, the divine Britney Jean Spears, and prepared for takeoff, hoping for the best.

The moment I took off from my forward outside edge, I knew something was different. I felt like Bastian on the wings of Falcor as I soared across the ice. My air position was tighter than it had ever been before. And the air felt surprisingly thin at an altitude likely never before achieved in the history of the sport.

It may be hard to believe, but that really was the first time that I landed my axel clean. And from that moment on, it became a reliable element in our program. Although I would never condone lying, I did learn a very important lesson that day. Surround yourself with people who challenge you. It is quite simply the best way to learn.

Oh, and never underestimate the celestial powers of the once-and-reigning pop princess.

But seriously, that lesson is one that I've carried with me throughout my professional life, helping me to change and grow as an educator. Those who commit to the path of lifelong learning, always striving to be better, are those I call my closest friends and collaborators. They also seem to be the people who lift me up and fill my cup, even when I'm not at my best.

That knowledge has also helped me to take charge of my anxiety and to manage my expectations for myself. Perhaps a little bit of healthy competition is the surest way to soar.

"I am many things:

a son, a brother, an uncle, a friend, an athlete, a cook, an author,

and being gay is just one part of who I am.

Brian Boitano

Mommy Dearest

My mother has never been one to hide her opinions. I knew from an early age that *All My Children* was masterpiece storytelling, while *One Life to Live* was a steaming pile of garbage. I knew that Julia Roberts was the greatest actress of all time, and that she was robbed of her *Pretty Woman* Oscar moment.

And through a number of off-handed comments made throughout my adolescence, I knew exactly how she felt about "the gays."

Three of those remarks in particular really stuck with me:

On Ellen Degeneres:

"I just can't believe people watch her show, knowing that she's *one of them*."

On meeting my first openly gay friend:

"He gives me the heebeegeebees."

On a friend's son coming out:

"I can't imagine how hard it is for her to have a freak for a son."

I'm Coming Out (Kinda)

We continued to improve our pairs elements at a surprising rate over the following year, and started to place in more and more competitions. It was at this point that my extended family, being the bunch of freeloaders that they were, finally started to get on board with my competitive skating career, including my relatively estranged, but considerably wealthy, uncle from the bougie shores of Shanty Bay.

And when I say "considerably wealthy" what I really mean is that he had piles of money markedly more impressive than Scrooge McDuck.

A former bigwig of the Toronto Stock Exchange, the guy was worth tens of millions of dollars. Twenty-five years prior, his wife would have been an absolute shoo-in for the cast of the Barrie iteration of *Real Housewives*. But unlike his self-centered mallard counterpart, my uncle had a strong sense of community, and readily made substantial contributions to countless local charities.

One such contribution was an annual donation to the Mariposa School of Skating. At the time, the club was one of the most successful elite training centres in the country, producing such notable alumni as Olympic Gold Medalist Meagan Duhamel, World Champion Jeffrey Buttle, and Canadian Silver Medalist (and the surely embarrassed) Christopher Mabee.

Along with a generous lump sum, my uncle would purchase extravagant table-service tickets to their annual charity gala every year. And when he found out about my Olympic figure skating aspirations, my uncle thought it would be a great opportunity for me to connect with a plethora of elite athletes.

So he invited my family to the show.

But there was a catch.

Like much of my extended family, he was a devoted Catholic and staunch Conservative. Although he enjoyed watching skating himself, he was highly skeptical of any man who would "willingly prance around in frilly outfits, just for attention." He had a sneaking suspicion that my participation in the sport was a sure sign of my alternative lifestyle. And he endeavored to ensure that my queerness would not leave a blemish on our otherwise pristine family name. Filthy Mudbloods.

My dad called me down to the basement after I returned from school one especially scorching summer afternoon (praise be to Madonna for central air on those hot as balls summer days), and shared the good news that we would be attending the Mariposa Charity Figure Skating Gala that August.

I nearly fainted on the spot.

I was already aware that my all-time favourite skater, Kurt Browning, would be featured in the show. But before I literally exploded with excitement, my dad revealed that the invitation was not without its conditions.

"Your uncle doesn't want to find out that you're gay."

I don't think I've ever felt a stronger sense of shame than in that moment. At the time, I was still trying to figure out my own identity. But before I had a chance to come to my own conclusions about who I was, I was told exactly who I should try not to be.

I felt so embarrassed.

On a fundamental level, it caused me to equate straight

with "loved and supported" and gay with "offensive and unloveable." And it delayed my coming out process by several years. I still don't think my parents fully comprehend how damaging this situation was to me as a young boy, already struggling to come to terms with my sexuality.

Looking back, I wish I had stood up for myself.

I can almost see it now. There I am, bounding to my feet with all the chutzpah of a young Fran Drescher. I smile, with my hip popped and my chest out, in my best *Working Girl* inspired power-stance. And I'm shouting at the top of my lungs, "I'm here. I'm queer. Get into it."

But that didn't happen.

I was just a kid. A kid with a dream. And at that point in time, the best way to achieve that dream was to go to the Mariposa Charity Figure Skating Gala with my unenlightened family, and to mingle with the best of the best.

So I bit my tongue and plastered on my most convincing poker face.

"That won't be a problem."

The question of my sexuality would continue to be a matter of contention between my uncle and I for years to come. And in many ways, it felt as if I was constantly being bribed to remain in my safe little closeted corner.

I stayed in the closet in exchange for a return invitation to the Mariposa Charity Gala the following year. I stayed in the closet in exchange for a month-long trip to England after my first year at Western University.

And my parents let it happen.

And their inaction spoke volumes.

When I finally was ready to share my truth with them, I had built up such a vast collection of negative experiences that I decided to come out to them over the phone. I was terrified that the situation would become physical, and decided to put my health and my heart first.

Thankfully, things never escalated to that point, and despite some initial tension (or rather an entire year during which I didn't speak to my mother), in recent years our relationship has become closer than ever.

My partner and I even joke that my mom likes him better than she likes me. I mean, if I dare to go home to visit without bringing Brad, I never hear the end of it. I think she especially enjoys having someone around who hasn't heard her stories a million times already.

Although we're probably getting close.

I never spoke to my uncle again after I came out, though. In fact, I'm not even entirely sure whether he found out about my decision to start living authentically before his death in the fall of 2020. And as insensitive as it may sound, I couldn't care less whether or not he knew.

In an ideal world, every queer-identifying individual would be able to come out in their own time, without the influence of outside forces (of evil…maniacal laugh ensues). But we don't live in an ideal world. Sometimes coming out waits for financial independence. Sometimes it waits for love. And sometimes it waits until after the Mariposa Charity Figure Skating Gala.

Regardless of what your coming out story looks like, you did it. And I'm so proud of you. Now, let's celebrate!

Sure Signs You Could Be Gay

~~Choosing to pursue figure skating instead of hockey.~~

~~Wearing your custom Jackson figure skates around the house.~~
(partially to break them in, and partially to live your *Top Model* fantasy)

~~Reaching euphoria with every sublime Sasha Cohen spiral
sequence.~~

~~Watching *Ice Princess* with your grandma on your birthday at the
local Famous Players.~~
(and again with your girlfriends after *Annie Warbucks* rehearsal)

~~Making a special trip to *Toys R Us* to purchase the new Tessa Virtue
Barbie.~~
(then writing to Mattel to demand they produce a Michelle Kwan *Barbie* stat)

~~Noticing how fine Evan Lysacek looks in his custom Vera Wang
bodysuit.~~

Finding yourself exclusively sexually attracted to men.

Why'd You Come in Here Lookin' Like That?

And there he was, in the flesh. A light dusting of chest hair covering his perfect perky pecs, and another strip connecting his belly button to his groin. He stood confidently in the middle of the brisk change room, nipples hard from the cold, filling out his skimpy tighty-whities better than any of the male models I'd ogled in that year's *SEARS Wish Book*.

No internet, remember? I had to get my kicks somehow.

Of course, I'd seen naked men before, in the swimming pool change rooms and on late-night television. But this was a moment of pure wish fulfillment. I'd been dreaming of this exact scenario since the moment I learned that I would be sharing a dressing room with the sexy senior from The Chatham Skating Club. I'd been undressing William with my eyes every day for a week as he glided around the rink, his muscular legs pumping against the frozen surface of the ice.

Take me back. If only I had a 1981 DeLorean.

My first memory of being attracted to another man was during my third year of the Ontario *Red Cross Swim Program*. My new coach was a blonde bombshell with an adorable button nose and a 100-Watt smile. I thought he was the most handsome man I had ever seen.

Although I didn't know it at the time, Matthew was my very first crush.

Every time he looked at me, I would feel this incredible sense of warmth moving through my body, all the way from the tips of my fingers to the bottom of my feet. And even now, when I think back to his face, I see it in this sort of nostalgic haze. Almost as if I'm viewing my own life through the lens of the Season One *RuPaul's Drag Race* filter.

Of course, this wouldn't be the last time I fell for a straight man. You know you've been there too. Forbidden fruit, amiright?

Picture it. Sicily. 1922. It was to be the final year that sisters Karolyn and Marianne would choreograph the Moore Skating Club Spring Carnival, and to mark the occasion, the club had hired a number of high-profile skaters to perform in the show. The impressive bill even included a performance from the notorious *Ice Men*, an all-male synchronized skating troup recognized as much for their comedic routines as for their collective accolades.

Boasting a number of the country's top skaters, Karolyn saw a perfect opportunity for me to engage in meaningful mentorship, and didn't hesitate to set up a meet-and-greet. She knew that I had been struggling with almost constant bullying that year, and was considering hanging up my skates. Perhaps a pseudo "big brother" would be just the encouragement I needed to persevere despite the judgment of adolescent jerks?

I found her backstage immediately following their rehearsal, and followed her into the change room.

But just as we walked in, the brawniest Ice Man of them all tore off his shirt and threw it into his gym bag. Oh. My. Lanta. I tried to avert my eyes and maintain my composure (it's probably less than ideal to sport a raging hard-on during a meet-and-greet), until I realized that the primo hunk of a man naked from the waist up was the very connection Karolyn wanted me to meet.

With his broad shoulders and washboard abs, Dylan

Moscovitch was nothing if not distracting. I tried to remember just one of the thousands of questions I had prepared the previous night, but standing in front of studly mcstud, I couldn't remember a single one. Instead, I stood there with my jaw on the floor, making indecipherable noises probably best described as a cracked out Pingu.

Thankfully, Dylan is essentially the Mister Rogers of the skating world, minus the oversized cardigan, and was as sweet as pie. And although we didn't make a lasting connection, seeing such an accomplished boy skater so happy and successful gave me just the glimmer of hope I needed. But it did leave me with one very important unanswered question. How many thousands of sit ups did he do every goddamn day to maintain those chiseled abs?

To be a fly on that home gym wall.

Of course, not every moment of attraction in my young life was quite so cinematic.

My family was left divided by the 2007 Canadian National Figure Skating Championships, as Jeffrey Buttle, Christopher Mabee, and Emmanuel Sandhu battled it out for the gold.

Without fail, my parents always cheered for the frontrunner, and as the three-time national champion, Emmanuel Sandhu fit the bill. My sister, on the other hand, was gaga for Jeffrey Buttle. He was blond and looked like a long-lost member of NSYNC. She was thirteen and hormonal. Need I say more?

But Christopher Mabee was my man. I had always admired Christoper for his incredible flexibility and his overtly theatrical performances. To me, he was part elite athlete and part Broadway baby. Every time he stepped out onto the ice, he brought such unflappable passion, and he always put on a show.

And I thought he was beautiful.

It wasn't the same sort of attraction I felt towards Matthew or Dylan, or would feel toward William. It wasn't more or less. It was just different. My thoughts of debauchery were kept (mostly) at bay, and instead replaced by reverence.

I studied every curvature of his lithe body as Christopher masterfully skated through a clean short program. He was lean and athletic, but muscular in all the right places. And his features were boyish, but also somehow rugged, with his dimpled chin and five-o'clock shadow. In a word, he was perfection. And I remember so vividly the pull to express that admiration aloud.

But even then, I knew that my admiration would be seen as unnatural. So I kept those thoughts to myself.

Until now, of course.

And I can only imagine that dear Christopher is becoming more and more mortified as he continues to read this section of my book, a deep scarlet blush creeping into those scruffy cheeks. Sorry not sorry. Suck it up, buttercup. You're beautiful, baby, and I've finally reached a point in my life where I'm not afraid to say it.

I think it's especially hard for queer men to fully come to terms with our sexuality. The message that being gay somehow means being less of a man still seems so deeply ingrained in modern society. I wish it was normalized for men to admire other men, for their minds and their talents. And also for their bodies.

I wish it was more normalized for men to experiment with other men. To feed our curiosity and to explore our sexuality.

I think things are changing, slowly but surely. And there's a glimmer of hope that things will be different for the generations of queer youth to come. But we still have a long road ahead.

Nothing happened, for the record. With William, I mean. Unless you consider a squawk of surprise, a quick pirouette, and the frantic slamming of a change room door to be a sexual fantasy in its own right.

Although I would have similar experiences of same-sex attraction throughout my early adolescence, it would still be several years before I started coming out, even to my closest friends (while woefully intoxicated at my 21st birthday party). And it would still be years still before I had my first intimate experience with a guy.

But you can bet that I made up for lost time.

Boff, Marry, Kick

Classique Edition

In case you're unfamiliar with the term, to "boff" means to "shag."
To "knock boots." To "make whoopee" or to dance the
"horizontal tango." You get the idea.

BOFF - Kurt Browning

> *The guy is married to a renowned ballerina. Some of that famed*
>
> *flexibility is bound to have rubbed off on him. Besides, I have a thing*
>
> *for bald guys.*

MARRY - Patrick Chan

> *He cooks. Enough said.*

KICK - Elvis Stojko

> *It's not that I don't like Elvis. Everybody likes Elvis. I love Elvis.*
>
> *But I have a feeling he likes it rough. Consensually (of course).*

"Ev and I have a great friendship on and off the ice,

and we have very similar work ethics.

We push each other, and we support each other.

I think the best quality to have is being able to laugh

and motivate each other.

Having someone there for you and vice versa is the biggest part."

Trennt Michaud

A (Totally Professional) Audition Notice

FEMALE PAIR SKATER WANTED

Who we are :

Joe Bainbridge is a rare find.

His love of classic literature and old MGM musicals is certainly uncommon for a fifteen-year-old boy, but endearing to most of his grandmother's friends.

You will find that his awkward banter and nervous laughter gradually become less grating. At least in theory.

He enjoys long walks on the beach, but hates the feeling of sand and is absolutely terrified of seagulls.

He also skates.

Position Summary :

Candidate will be required to perform choreographed routines containing necessary elements of the pre-novice level.

She will be repetitively thrown several feet into the air with the expectation of landing on her feet. Mostly.

Position will include occasional appearances at spring carnivals and charity galas. Usually by invitation.

Opulent heavily sequined costume is non-negotiable.

Necessary Skills :

Must be able to jump (but not too high), spin (but not too fast), and hold incredibly awkward body positions for indeterminate amounts of time.

Clairvoyance is a major asset to help anticipate last-minute changes in choreography due to her partner's stress-induced memory loss.

In case of error, must be able to fall with all the grace of a wild gazelle with thirty years of ballet training.

Spatial awareness is essential in order to avoid accidental skewering or decapitation.

Preference will be given to candidates with a vested interest (read obsession) with *Beauty and the Geek*.

Fans of *Billy Talent* need not apply.

Until It's Time for You to Go

Alexa and I quickly started losing momentum after narrowly missing the podium at our second regionals during our third year together as a pair. And after much consideration, we decided to go our separate ways. Alexa had fallen in love with synchronized skating and wanted to spend more time training with her teammates in Chatham. And I was happy for her.

There would be no trial separation this time around. It was a quick and amicable split. There was no lengthy custody battle, and we divided our assets equally. If you can count our handful of novelty plushies as "assets," that is. And in a gesture of good will, I even let Alexa keep the turquoise finger gloves she had unceremoniously swiped from me months prior.

But deep down, I was heartbroken.

I had fallen head-over-heels in love with pair skating, and I wasn't ready to let go. So Deb and I spent the next several weeks auditioning new potential partners.

First there was Alicia. With a lithe and lanky physicality, and the flexibility of a freak show contortionist, she was a pair skating dream. And her nickname "the jumping bean" was certainly no exaggeration. She threw herself into the air with reckless abandon, yet somehow managed to stick the landing and stay on her feet every single time.

There was only one problem. Her bodily control during lifts and twists was terrifying. She flopped around like a rag doll. And the unpredictability of her seemingly possessed extremities made for some close calls. I spent nearly as much time dodging her flailing blades as anything else. So at the risk of suffering a fate similar to Marie Antionette, I decided to pass on the partnership.

Mackenzie was next. She looked like Tessa Virtue, gliding in with her tight bun and porcelain features. And much like Tessa, the girl had a fabulous sense of style. Her cream chiffon skating dress with that collared hand-woven lace neckline was to die for. I couldn't help but dream about how handsome a couple we would make atop that Olympic podium.

But the dream ended there. The only thing more stiff than

Mackenzie's posture was her personality. Now don't get me wrong, she was a very nice girl. But we had absolutely zero chemistry. For one, she was totally clueless when it came to the life and times of Lorelei and Rory Gilmore, and her favourite Disney movie was *Home on the Range* (puke). But perhaps the biggest red flag of all? She thought sour keys were gross. How very dare.

Go directly to jail. Do not pass go. Do not collect $200.

I'm sorry to say that the rest of the auditions were equally as unsatisfying. Or worse, entirely forgettable. But disappointing audition after disappointing audition, I came to realize that all of the skaters we tried out had one single shortcoming in common.

None of them were Alexa.

Finding the perfect partner is like getting hit by lightning. And with Alexa, our connection was electrifying and rare. What were the chances that feeling would strike yet again? Especially considering Jonathan Van Ness wouldn't take up the sport for another fifteen years. Now there's a match made in heaven. I wonder if he's busy now? I mean, think of all we could accomplish in four years with a little bit of talent and a whole lot of extra.

Watch out, Milan 2026.

Bainbridge and VanNess are ready to slay.

But since my favourite *Queer Eye* queer was unavailable at the time, I decided to make my highly anticipated (read as utterly dreaded) return to singles skating.

But my heart just wasn't in it.

And as my passion for the sport waned, so did my skill. My jumps became less consistent. I lost so much of my flexibility. And my lack of energy was completely uncharacteristic. So I scaled back my pre-novice program and entered into a handful of local competitions at the junior level.

But as I walked into the change room on the day of my first competition that season, I realized that there was one glaring difference between me and the other competitors. All of the other boys in my flight were about half a foot shorter and at least five years younger than me.

Fuck.

I felt like an ungainly Robbie Coltrane (Hagrid from *Harry Potter*) towering over a crew of young Macauley Culkins. You know, in his cute *Home Alone* period. Not his dismaying meth-chic days.

I felt absolutely humiliated.

And in perhaps the most insolent diva moment of my entire life, I refused to skate.

But my coach wasn't going to give up that easily. She was able to pull some strings and enter me as a last-minute addition to the pre-novice group, who were competing concurrently on the other ice. That Hail Mary move, however, would put me in a stressful situation, to say the least.

For starters, I would have to perform a program that I hadn't practiced in months, and I would be attempting jumps that I hadn't landed consistently all season. I had already missed the warm-up, and would have to skate my program cold. Not to mention, Deb was tied to another skater on the other ice, so I would have to manage it all without my coach.

No big deal, right?

But as I stood in line watching the other skaters perform their routines with obvious gusto, my heart started to beat faster and faster. I tried to visualize myself skating through my pre-novice program, but was at a complete loss. It seemed so alien and unfamiliar. And instead, I imagined myself floundering through a series of disconnected elements, fall after excruciating fall, a shrill Piper Laurie chanting in my head, "They're all going to laugh at you." And all of a sudden, I couldn't breathe.

How cute.

Baby's first panic attack.

Without a word to anyone, I quickly escaped to the empty change rooms and locked myself in the bathroom. Ah. It seems we've been here before. This time, minus Nick and his pre-teen mafia. Plus one blubbering mess. I sat on the toilet with my head between my knees until my breathing finally started to return to normal. Then I quickly found my confused parents in the crowd and enjoyed a very awkward silence on the thankfully short drive home to Corunna.

The next day, I withdrew from all of my remaining appearances that season.

This queen bitch was taking an indefinite hiatus.

"Being different in any way, no matter what that difference is,

in this case, sexual orientation,

doesn't preclude you from belonging to whatever

community of sport that you're a part of."

Paul Poirier

Somewhere (There's a Place for Us)

Although I continued to skate recreationally for the remainder of the season, I cut back on almost all of my private lessons and off-ice training. And without all the time spent preparing for competition, I finally had time to pursue other interests.

So when I came across an audition notice for a local production of *Godspell,* I decided to take the leap. I had been singing in my church choir for several years, and no one seemed to complain about my voice. At least not to my face. Besides, Tara Lipinski had effortlessly made the transition to television acting following her gold medal moment. If Tara could book *Sabrina the Teenage Witch* then surely I had a shot at Sarnia stardom.

And guess what? I booked it.

I mean, I was a teenage boy living in an aging rural community auditioning for a community theatre production of an outdated musical about bible parables with glossy production numbers and enough jazz hands to make Bob Fosse shed a posthumous tear of joy. So the competition was just as stiff as you could imagine.

Still, it was a much needed boost of confidence after my experience at the competition to end all competitions. And even more importantly, I found something I didn't even know I'd been looking for at the time: a community of people just like me.

Our first *Godspell* rehearsal was spent getting to know the cast and crew through a series of ice-breakers and trust-building activities. All of the teenagers in the cast, eight of us in total, were grouped together. Our first discussion was led by our petite but plucky leader, Aaron Bergeron.

Aaron would be portraying Jesus in our show.

"I can't wait to get to know each and every one of you." He had all the charm and humility of a young Sally Field. And we liked him. We really liked him. "My boyfriend and I moved here a few months ago to study early childhood education at Lambton College, so we're new to the area."

Remember that moment in *The Wizard of Oz* when

Dorothy steps out of her house and into Munchkinland, and in an instant, everything changes from dull sepia tone to vibrant technicolour? That's how I felt at that first rehearsal. I know, I know. How cliché. But we've already established that I'm as gay as the day is long. Let me have my Judy Garland fantasy.

Aaron was the first out gay man I had met "in real life." And in an instant, he shattered all of my preconceived notions about what it meant to be a homosexual. Maybe my mother was wrong about gay people after all. Aaron was happy. He was bright and successful and confident. But most of all, he was loved.

And as far as I could tell, he seemed to be loved for his queerness, not in spite of it.

Now in reality, I'm sure Aaron was not really the first gay man that I'd crossed paths with. The figure skating world was full of more Betties than a Kylie Minogue concert during World Pride. But due to the value of traditional masculinity in competitive skating, so many of these men were forced to negotiate their queerness and to supress their personality in order to "pass" as straight.

But I never felt that way during my experiences with community theatre. Despite portraying the Messiah on stage, Aaron was never asked to quell his animated lisp or "butch it up." Instead, he seemed to wear his queerness like a badge of honour.

And he wasn't the only one. Our choreographer, Megan Hadley, was an out lesbian, and her life-partner, Val, built all of our sets. At the time, their penchant for leather seemed in stark contrast to their strong maternal instincts. It took me longer than I'd like to admit to learn that clothes do not, in fact, make the man. Besides, leather is *Totally Hot*. Just ask Dame Olivia Newton-John.

There was only one other boy my age in the cast. And although Grant Pettypiece was still in the closet at school, he felt comfortable enough to reveal his authentic self during our *Godspell* rehearsals. He gushed about the cute boy in his history class to just about anyone who was willing to listen (or simply unable to escape fast enough to evade his neverending stories of teenage lust).

And that's the most incredible thing about Aaron. And Megan. And Grant. They weren't just figureheads. They were people. With careers and partners. And lives.

And that, to me, is a very important differentiation.

Of course visibility matters. But really, it's only the first step towards inclusivity. I hope that in the years to come, figure skating becomes a genuinely safe space for queer youth. A space where flamboyant youngsters can let their freak flags fly, and be celebrated for their differences.

I hope that figure skating fosters a greater sense of community and connection. That the work to make figure skating a sport "for everyone" encourages more young boys to give it a shot, and eliminates the "token male" at skating clubs across the country.

And I hope that athletes start to move beyond "coming out" and towards living authentically and openly. Being queer isn't just a moment. It's a lifetime. The importance of seeing what comes next is absolutely crucial for baby queers.

I mean, the pictures that pretty Paul Paurier posts to his social media of him and his handsome beau making out in skimpy white speedos may not be featured in his "CBC Olympic Spotlight" any time soon.

But we can all dare to dream.

"To be surrounded by a good support system as a teen

is key in my opinion. Whether you're an athlete or a student,

having an adult who believes in you and can give you advice

and wisdom that is coming from a place of experience

is an incredible asset to help guide you through your young life."

Tara Lipinski

When I Grow Up

After hanging up my skates at the beginning of the tenth grade, I decided it was time to pursue a new dream. And since Emma, Geri, Mel C, Mel B, and Victoria had gone their separate ways years prior, my prospects of becoming the sixth Spice Girl seemed dismal. So I decided to throw my energy into becoming a teacher. Whether that decision was prompted by my positive experiences with peer tutoring the previous year or my infatuation with my absolute zaddy of a ninth grade mathematics teacher is really anybody's guess.

Seriously, the guy was an adonis. He was the spitting image of Juan Carlos Salazar, the sexy barrel-chested star of *Latin Lover*, a late-night softcore telanovella that spurred the sexual awakening of countless gay teens in the early 2000s. Do yourself a favour and Google Juan Carlos. I'll give you a few minutes to, well, you know. And we'll regroup here in ten.

Regardless of my true motivation, I was certain that

teaching was the perfect career for me, and I began to seek out new opportunities to bestow my considerable knowledge on the younger generation. And at the advanced age of sixteen, I would clearly be an asset to just about any milieu lucky enough to be graced with my presence.

Nevertheless, I decided to start with what I knew best: figure skating. Ever since my favourite sitcom, *Sabrina the Teenage Witch*, had ended its seven-year reign on The WB, my Friday nights were unusually free. So, I accepted a volunteer position as a junior coach at my alma mater, the Moore Skating Club, and began working with a group of the youngest skaters on the ice.

It didn't take long for me to come to the conclusion that working with kindergarten aged children was not my forte. For one thing, they tend to cry. A lot. And rather than attempting to console the little darlings, my natural response was always to cry right along with them. Remember that thing about crying all the time? Yup. Still a thing. It was a dumpster fire.

Furthermore, trying to maintain a thoughtful conversation with a four-year-old about which member of NSYNC is the dreamiest is an exercise in futility. Justin. The answer is clearly Justin. But Susie didn't seem to have a clue.

That's not to say that there weren't any success stories in my illustrious career as a coach. One of my most successful students spent years performing with *Disney on Ice,* and I would attend the tour every time she was in town, skating as Wendy or Rapunzel or even, on occasion, Belle. My favourite of all the princesses. I always joke that I taught her everything she knows. And then she threw all that shite out the window and really learned how to skate.

But overall, I learned that I didn't have the energy nor the disposition to spend the rest of my days negotiating micro-tantrums with preschoolers. The nail in the coffin was a traumatic experience backstage at the Moore Skating Club's annual spring ice carnival.

If there's one thing you need to know about the backstage area of the Moore Skating Club's spring ice carnival, it's that it's a chaotic mess. Think of a Metallica concert mosh pit. But with overtired children. Wearing knives on their feet.

So there I was, trying to wrangle a hoard of screaming children, all donning recently sharpened foot knives. And I had but thirty seconds to line them all up for their *Fantasia* inspired routine. In their correct order. In the dark.

Now, ice carnival costumes are truly the epitome of "best drag." In this case, the hoard of "elephants" in question were all wearing fitted grey bodysuits with sparkly pink tutus overtop, pastel headbands with large styrofoam ears attached (each of which was approximately the size of a beach ball) inordinately tethered to each tiny ponytail with an altogether excessive number of bobby pins, and flowing silk scarves in each tiny gloved hand to create the illusion of an extended trunk. In the true sense of the word, these elephants were extra.

Moments before they stepped onto the ice, one of my more inelegant elephants dropped her silk scarf, and as her bottom lip began to tremble, I recognized the early signs of a major meltdown. Thinking on my feet, I whispered to the remaining pachyderms to hold still, and I reached down to retrieve her discarded trunk.

You can probably see where this is going.

As an over enthusiastic elephant raced towards her moment in the spotlight, her blade glided directly over my right ring finger. I tried my very best not to scream like Regina George after she finds out that the Kalteen bars she has been consuming are the cause of her rapid weight gain, and raised my hand to assess the damage.

By some act of Beyonce, the injury was less severe than I had expected, with minimal blood and only a thin line of indentation beneath my nail. But the damage was done. I could never become a hand model now. I decided then and there that my child-wrangling days were over, at the risk of possible amputation down the line.

Years later, when I applied to Western University's Faculty of Education, I made an informed decision to avoid primary and junior teaching as unapologetically as Jake Gyllenhaal apparently avoids showering. Meh. I still wouldn't kick him out of bed.

But in working with young adults, I found my true vocation in life. Zoomers get a lot of flack for being too technology dependent and for making outrageously stupid decisions, seemingly for no apparent reason. I mean, we all remember the Tide Pod challenge, right? But in my opinion, they are the most resilient generation of all.

Their formative years were stilted by the impacts of the COVID-19 pandemic, yet they still maintain incredible altruistic integrity, from bringing numerous racial issues to the forefront of global media to insisting fair wages for all regardless of gender or sexual orientation. I'm truly in awe of my students.

They rock my world every day, and someday I know they'll change yours.

Manufacturing Moments of Public Embarrassment

sponsored by Big Brother Businesses

In order to establish a meaningful and lasting relationship with a younger brother or sister, it is absolutely crucial for an older sibling to completely traumatize their successors via repeated moments of public humiliation.

As an award-watching author, let me share some helpful pointers:

Be creative. Try referring to your sibling using a series of inane and unflattering nicknames. loudly at the grocery store or even in front of their friends at school. Among others, these nicknames could include Missy Gog, Gump Veroo, or Jeery Candle.

Declassify. Try "accidentally" revealing a secret your sibling has shared with you at an inopportune moment. This could be easily accomplished in casual conversation, or through self-publishing a book referencing their childhood crushes and figure skating fails.

Commit to your art. Try audibly wailing in a packed movie theatre, loudly enough for a concerned Cineplex employee to ask if you would like some water. Or a Xanax. Selecting a pivotal moment in the film is crucial to this effort, like when Andy decides to give up his toys at the end of *Toy Story 3*.

As a disclaimer, this list is by no means comprehensive.

That would be another book entirely.

"I just try to touch people's hearts in a way through skating,

so they're not just witnessing a performance,

they're feeling a performance and they're a part of it."

Scott Hamilton

Paparazzi

My relationship with my sister started out rocky. And at this point in my life, I'm willing to take full responsibility for that.

I vividly remember the day my parents told me that there would be a new addition to our family. To say I was not pleased would be an understatement of epic proportions. I wanted a baby sister like I wanted a hole in my head. And based on how often my dad seemed to use this saying growing up, that was not a lot.

Sharing my parents' love and affection with some bald little parasite was not what I signed up for, and in an act of defiance, I was a complete prick towards her for the first several years of her life. Early on, I came up with a completely infallible way to manipulate her into doing whatever I wanted her to do.

One day, while riding to the movies in the back of my grandmother's hefty maroon Crown Victoria, I casually mentioned a truly terrifying notion. "Did you know that if your longest hair falls out, you'll die instantly?" A look of absolute horror crossed my sister's face. "But how do you know which hair is the longest?" I only shrugged, and looked out the window. "I guess you don't." And with that brief exchange, the groundwork had been laid.

The next time Sarah refused to let me have the monkey juice box holder (clearly the greatest of all the animal juice box holders), I simply reached out and grabbed a single strand of hair from under her headband, and started to pull. "I hope this isn't the longest one." It worked like a charm. The monkey juicebox was mine, and this seedy manipulation became a common occurrence.

I know, I know. I was truly an evil mastermind. I mean, how did I even come up with such a grotesque conspiracy? All I can say is that I'm not the villain I once was. And I'm sorry for my former wicked ways. But that's not to say that my youngest sibling was entirely blameless.

Just a few years ago, my parents and I were looking through vintage family photos, and I noticed something peculiar. In nearly every picture of my sister and I prior to 1995, I appear to be shoving an apple in her face. Now, my initial thought was that it must have been some strange reference to *Snow White and the Seven*

Dwarfs, my favourite movie at the time. Did I (not so secretly) want to poison my own sister?

But when I asked my mom about the strange phenomenon, she hardly seemed fazed. During teething, I was apparently my sister's favourite chew toy. She bit me so hard and so often that I took up the habit of carrying apples with me wherever I went. "They were for your protection," my mom admitted with a shrug. Forget about "Charlie Bit Me." My sister had the gag perfected long before that video went viral.

In fact, that fall when I started kindergarten, the problem had become so bad that my body was absolutely covered with tiny bruises and puncture wounds. Thinking they were the result of abuse or negligence, my primary teacher went so far as to call Child Protective Services. Boy were they surprised to find that my baby sister was the true source of such despicable villainy.

Yet against all the odds, somehow we grew to become the very best of friends in our teenage and adult years. In fact, we often joke that we're essentially the same person. We bonded over our unhealthy obsession with *Gilmore Girls*. I'd like to think that I'm the droll Lorelai to her stalwart Emily. We bonded over our distaste for team sports. There are only a handful of situations where I actually enjoy having balls hurtling toward my face.

But perhaps our most memorable early moment of sibling bonding was our position as committed figure skating paparazzi. After the first Mariposa Charity Gala performance, my uncle mentioned offhandedly that our ticket included an exclusive cocktail reception with the cast. He would not be attending, of course. Clearly, the entire thing was beneath him. But my sister and I were absolutely gagging at the opportunity.

We spent the night socializing with the likes of Jeff Buttle and Joanie Rochette. Well, not socializing, per se. We both stood just outside of their actual conversations until one of them noticed us creeping and sent us on our way with an autograph and a selfie. Same thing, right?

Did I mention that my sister and I are both painfully shy? There is no "outgoing one" in our sibling pair. It's real fun. But despite our social anxiety, we had a blast. And we couldn't wait to mingle with industry bigwigs again the following year.

Over the years, we had the pleasure of rubbing shoulders with Elvis Stojko, Jennifer Robinson, and even Kurt Browning. But my favourite story is the time we met the two most decorated figure skaters of all time.

My husband refers to this story as the day I broke my mother's heart.

He's not wrong.

The creative arts floor at Western University wasn't always the best place for me to study. For whatever reason, learning about differential equations to the calming sounds of Kesha and projectile vomiting, while nice in theory, wasn't doing my grades any favours. So when finals came along, I made my way back to Sarnia after my final day of classes to study in peace.

It just so happened that my arrival also coincided with my mother's birthday, and her favourite way to celebrate had always been to venture to Degroots to pick out our family Christmas tree. Now, this particular holiday tradition had never been my favourite, so I was happy to have an excuse to politely decline. I simply had too much studying to do. My sister followed suit. After a long day of work at No Frills, she was overdue for a nap.

But ten minutes after my parents left to live out their *Hallmark Channel* dreams, I received a text that would change my life forever. Or at least for that afternoon. Tessa Virtue and Scott Moir were passing through on a province-wide tour, and would be making a stop at *The Bookkeeper* to sign copies of their new release.

I showed my sister the text. "We shouldn't." She bit her lip, sheepishly. "We couldn't."

We did.

Not an hour later, my sister and I were home with our signed copies of *Tessa and Scott: Our Journey from Childhood Dream to Gold*, and smiles bigger than little orphan Annie when she realizes that someday, in the not too distant future, Daddy Warbucks will pass on, and she'll be richer than a post-settlement Mackenzie Scott. Well, maybe they weren't that big.

I have always been completely unable to lie. Seriously. Just ask Brad. I've ruined many a surprise with my most honourable undoing. So when my parents returned home later that day, I spilled the beans almost immediately. And my mother responded in a manner perfectly befitting of the master of guilt herself.

She could have yelled. She could have cried. But either of those options would have been better than the wounded look that crossed her face. "I would have liked to come too."

Ruthless. Just ruthless.

Kiss, Marry, Kick

Canadian Pairs Edition

I know, I know. Kick? But I refuse to go down for homicidal intent. I wouldn't make it in the slammer. I'm much too pretty.

KISS - Michael Marinaro

I trust Kirsten's opinion. She has impeccable taste. I mean, have you seen her bejeweled 2022 Olympic outfit? The way it shimmers is just stunning. Also, those lips!

MARRY - Trennt Michaud

Recording and editing his own podcast while maintaining a charitable clothing company? The guy is a true renaissance man. And you should see him with kids! Definitely husband material.

KICK - Eric Radford

This one was an easy choice. You did my girl wrong, Eric. #JusticeForMeagan And crashing the 2022 Olympic team? In the words of Stephanie Tanner, "How Rude!"

So Emotional

I've always had problems with empathy. But wait, before you go putting my name on some *Hunting an Internet Killer* social media watch list, I'm no Joe Golberg. It's not a lack of empathy I struggle with, but rather a sort of displaced abundance of feeling, sometimes for things that have very little to do with me. It's almost like "the butterfly effect," but on a very personal level. Even the smallest fluctuations in emotion can throw me into a spiral.

One of my earliest memories of this abundance of feeling happened at my sister's first figure skating competition. It was the first time I realized that my sister was beautiful. Until that point, Sarah had been wearing my aunt's hand-me-down skating outfits during our practices and showcases. But for her competitive debut, those old rags simply wouldn't do. We all know that figure skating isn't a blue-collar sport. Just ask Tonya Harding.

For her first appearance on the circuit, Sarah would need a costume befitting of a true ice princess. And once again, with the threat of layoffs looming at my dad's work, our local skating community came to the rescue, and my sister was provided with a stunning pink and silver dress for a more than reasonable price. It shimmered dramatically under the harsh arena lighting, perfectly complementing the glitter-dusted butterfly clips orbiting her rag-curled ponytail.

She looked like a pop star, and with her adorable "Girls Just Wanna Have Fun" routine, she seemed poised to storm the podium. But as soon as her music started, my sister let her nerves get the best of her, and the program itself was a bit of a disaster. I felt a shock wave of emotion with each error. And by the end of her performance, despite having never left the arena bleachers, I felt completely exhausted.

My sister definitely shed a tear or two after receiving her scores and finishing second-to-last in her group. But just like her favourite drag icon Jinkx Monsoon, it was soon water off a duck's back, and she was totally over it by the time we made it to lunch. I, on the other hand, felt miserable for the remainder of the day.

Projecting my own feelings of disappointment onto my

sister, I spent hours obsessing over ways to cheer her up. After much consideration, I decided that a spontaneous trip to Disney World seemed like the most suitable response. After all, I had almost fifty dollars saved from my recent birthday. But convincing my acrophobic mother to step on a "flying metal deathtrap," otherwise known as an airplane, would be an exercise in futility. So I eventually settled on purchasing a stylish and dramatically overpriced plush mermaid from the competition gift shop.

And she loved it.

My sister didn't need cheering up by the time I made my not-so grand gesture. But it did add a positive spin to her memory of that day. And it was a token which she carried with her to every single competition thereafter.

In that respect, my displaced abundance of feeling isn't always a bad thing. In many ways, I think it's what makes me such a thoughtful and generous friend. But on the other hand, sometimes this heightened sense of empathy also wears on me, and causes me to react in ways that aren't always appropriate to the circumstances.

Devouring full broadcasts of International Skating Union

Championships on CBC Gem is sometimes the only guaranteed way to pull me out of a funk. I can kill a Friday night (and Saturday morning, and Saturday afternoon) no problem, watching flight after flight of earnest competitors, starting with an assortment of relative unknowns before working up to the medal favourites.

Sure, I could defaut to the highlights shown on regular broadcast television. But skating is skating, right? (And if you aren't watching *Untucked,* you're only getting half the story).

Sometimes my partner will join me during the later flights of skaters. But his knowledge of figure skating is minimal. I mean, he laughed hysterically after finding out that "salchow" and "flying camel" are technical terms used within the sport. And now he tends to make up weird, animal-inspired monikers for all of the elements. Which is kind of hilarious. Sometimes.

For the most part, though, televised skating gives me an opportunity to spend quality time with me, myself, and I. And with a selection of my closest friends. Friends who often live thousands of miles away. Friends who never call. Friends who, in most regards, have no idea that I even exist.

Ok, fine. I'm talking about the athletes themselves.

Yes, I call them my friends. Sue me.

I feel such a sense of connectedness to my favourite skaters. Perhaps that connection is a false sense of knowing forged through social media. Perhaps it's latent nostalgia for my own nearly forgotten figure skating dreams. Or perhaps it's just another manifestation of that aforementioned displaced abundance of feeling. But most likely, it's a combination of all three.

But regardless of the source, this strong sense of connectedness is something that often impacts me in a substantial way. I share in a skater's triumphs, but also in their defeats and disappointments. And I carry that baggage with me throughout my day (my week, my month, or even my year).

The day before the 2022 Canadian National Figure Skating Championships, my husband and I lost our beloved cat, Isaac. His passing wasn't exactly a surprise, seeing as he was just shy of a million years old in cat years. But regardless of the circumstances, it's never easy losing a pet. They really are members of the family. And my emotions were all over the place.

So as my favourite pairs team, Trennt Michaud and Evelyn Walsh, took the ice for their short program, I was already in tears. And I don't mean a delicate twinkle of moisture in the corner of my eye. I mean I was ugly crying. Like Rachel McAdams in *The Notebook*. Except I hate birds.

After a difficult season of injury and inconsistency, there was so much riding on this single competition, including a spot on the Beijing Olympic Team. So my stomach was in knots for the entirety of the routine. It was truly the longest 2 minutes and 40 seconds of my entire life. But as Trennt and Evelyn nailed element after element, I finally eased into my nerves. And by the end of their flawless performance, a whole new slew of tears found their way down my cheeks. This time, tears of happiness.

These friends of mine always had a way of stepping up when it mattered the most.

The entire operation, including my own personal emotional rollercoaster, would be repeated once again just a day later, for a season's best long program. And the wonder twins finished in second place overall, just behind veteran duo Kirsten Moore-

Towers and Michael Marinaro. I felt pure joy for the first time in months, since our dear Isaac had first taken ill.

I was so proud. And I felt such a strong sense of mutual achievement. I mean, I'm fairly certain my constant vocal encouragement from our spare room (also known as my makeshift virtual classroom during this time) was the real clincher.

We did it.

But of course, if the past two years had been any indication, I should have learned to expect the unexpected. I seemed to have forgotten that rule number one of living in a pandemic is to never let your guard down. And when the Olympic team was announced the following morning, Trennt and Evelyn were inexplicably absent from the list.

I felt personally affronted, and said as much to just about anyone who was willing to listen. And I felt like it was my personal responsibility to right this cruel injustice. But I had a feeling that dramatically overpriced plush mermaids just weren't going to cut it this time. Regardless of how fabulous their shimmering sequined tails may be.

I obviously didn't have much clout to reverse the decision, seeing as my covert connections at the International Skating Union had fallen into disrepair since leaving the sport. And due to the fact that they were largely imaginary in the first place. Besides, staging a national-level coup to get my way would probably fall under that whole "reacting in ways inappropriate to the circumstances" thing. But I still felt like I needed to do something.

After a week sitting in my emotions, I channeled my abundance of feeling into a lesson at school titled "Athletes in Action." I focused on the myriad of ways that the pair had already made their mark on the sport, from Trennt's charitable initiatives to Eveleyn's balance between education and elite-level athletics. And just like Bagga Chipz, I felt "Much Betta."

As a teacher, I have the opportunity to engage in meaningful discussion every day with large groups of critical thinkers. I have the opportunity to share issues and ideas that are important to me, and to instill in my students a desire for fairness and accountability.

Just two weeks later, I had another major revelation: I also have the ability to force an entire class of fourteen-year-olds to watch the Four Continents with me at a whim.

Oh, yes. My power is truly awe-inspiring.

But I digress.

We may not all have the power or platform we desire, but we all have a voice. Use your voice to share your passions, to stand up for what you believe in, and to make change. That's one reaction that is never inappropriate to the circumstances.

And if you're anything like me, your hyper-sensitive soul will thank you.

A Glossary of (Olympic Season) Terms

darling dud: a crowd-pleasing program that for one reason or another fails to resonate with international judges; especially common in ice dance

displacer chaser: an athlete returning to competition during an Olympic year who puloins an Olympic team spot from a more deserving athlete (see also *fomo dodo*)

fomo dodo: a formerly-retired athlete that returns to competition during an Olympic year in a hopeless attempt to relive their Olympic glory days (see also *displacer chaser*)

podium pretension: valuing a skater or pair for their place on the podium rather than for their individual performance; especially bothersome when a skater or pair achieves a personal best

Who Says You Can't Go Home

It's been nearly ten years since I've laced up my skates, and most days it feels as if my days of competitive figure skating were in another life entirely. On those days, my chronic hip and knee pain seem to be the only lasting reminders of my glory days.

Ouch.

But once in a blue moon, when the planets align and all five of the Spice Girls are on speaking terms, I'm nearly able to convince myself that I could do it all again.

Some days I can feel the pull of the ice deep within my bones. And today is one of those days.

I can almost make out the rhythmic scraping of metal on ice as the skaters begin their practice. All broad gliding strokes and deep frenzied crossovers.

Never skip the warm-up.

I can almost feel the cold air teasing the sensitive sliver of skin between my shirt sleeve and my gloves. My finger-looped undershirt lay neglected on the dressing room floor.

Again.

I can almost taste the sharp bitterness of a carefully concealed sour key meeting my tongue.

No food on the ice.

Sometimes, my soul longs to know what it would feel like to fly once more.

But how long would it take to recover my skills? Would it be like riding a bike? Or would my nearly early-middle-aged body get so twisted and tangled that even Charlotte would have trouble untangling my portly web of limbs?

I suppose there's only one way to know for sure.

Do I dare?

"This is Bayview Arena. How may I direct your call?"

"Oh, hi. Yes. I'd like to book some private ice time.

Acknowledgements

Deb. I learned everything I know about figure skating under your careful guidance. You taught me how to fly, but the life lessons and unconditional support are what made you a truly one-of-a-kind coach.

Alexa. For being the best partner-in-crime a baby queer could ask for. You always pushed me to be the best that I could be, as a skater and as a friend. And your constant shenanigans always made practice a riot.

Dad. Even at the worst of times, I never doubted your love. You always led by example, and taught me the true value of hard work. I love you, but you are definitely a Miranda.

Mom. The sacrifices you made for me never went unnoticed. We had our struggles, and I never thought you would become one of my strongest supporters. But here we are. I love you, and I'm making peace that Brad is your favourite.

Sarah. My beautiful sister. We have been through so much together. You are my greatest ally and my best friend. I'm sorry for torturing you for the sake of entertainment. And torturing you for the sake of, well, laziness. You are the Rory to my Paris.

Tina and Trennt and Jamie and Doug. Thank you for taking the time to read earlier versions of *Queer Musings of a One-Time Boy Skater*. Your thoughtful feedback helped to elevate this project to a new level of awesomesauce.

Adelle. You are the most talented person I know, and the cover art you created for this book is so full of love. Despite my complete inability to make decisions, you somehow always knew exactly what I wanted, usually before I did. Get out of my head.

Brad. By the time this book is finally published, you will be my husband. And I have no doubts that we'll already be acting like an old married couple, spending our Saturday nights at *Home Depot* or *Bed, Bath and Beyond* and bickering about what to have for dinner. So…same? Your love is the best thing that ever happened to me, and I am forever grateful we met. This is for you.

Glossary

Abby Lee Miller: the devil incarnate

All My Children: masterpiece stroytelling

Alyssa Edwards: an insanely quotable contestant featured on the
fifth season of *RuPaul's Drag Race* and in the second season of
Rupaul's All Stars Drag Race; often referred to as "the most beautiful
creature on the planet" (By me. I'm the one who said that.)

Annie Warbucks: sole heir to the entire Warbucks estate; also, an
offensively bad sequel to the original Broadway musical

Bagga Chipz: a busty and brazen contestant on the first season of
Rupaul's Drag Race UK; coined the phrase "much betta," which has
since become drag race canon

Beauty and the Beast: the first animated feature to be nominated
for *Best Picture* at the Oscars; objectively the best Disney film

Beauty and the Geek: a 2005 reality series produced by Ashton
Kutcher featuring an endearing cast of socially awkward (and often
surprisingly handsome) men alongside their "pretty but dumb"

female counterparts (usually models)

Belle: a bookworm and adventurer; objectively the best Disney Princess (voiced by the sweet-as-pie Paige O'Hara)

Beyonce: queen

Billy Talent: gross

Bob Fosse: Miss Patty's favourite choreographer

Britney Spears: the princess of pop; wanted a Bugatti and a Maserati and a hot body, so she worked (bitch)

Call of Duty hard pass

"Charlie Bit Me": a viral video featuring two adorable young British boys; "That hurt, and it's still hurting" (Not to be confused with "Still Hurting," the emotionally devastating number from Jason Robert Brown's *The Last Five Years*.)

chemical valley: a small area in Sarnia containing approximately forty percent of the Canadian chemical industry; known for being one of the most polluted hotspots in the country (Yay.)

Cher: the OG pop diva and queer icon; does an unbelievable Chad Michaels impression (see also "babe")

Coffee Lodge: rustic Starbucks

Crown Victoria: a very unsexy car

Degroots: a nursery in Sarnia that locals invariably mistake for a larger chain (see also Coffee Lodge and Farley's Funhouse)

Dorothy Hamill: 1976 Olympic Figure Skating champion; equally known for her cheeky pixie cut as for her actual skating skills

Ellen Degeneres: one of us

European Waltz: a triggering series of three-turns and edges

Exorcist, The: my grandma's favourite documentary

Faerie Tale Theatre: Shelley Duvall's incredibly self-indulgent but overall enjoyable series of hour-long fairy tale adaptations starring an unbelievable slew of gay icons, from Jennifer Beals to Leslie Ann Warren to Bernadette Peters

Farley's Funhouse: like an uninsurable Chuck E Cheese

Fire on Ice: the seminal (an sole) memoir released by legendary figure skating artist Sasha Cohen

Four Continents: an International Skating Union event featuring competitors from Canada, China, Japan, and the USA; often overshadowed by the World Figure Skating Championships and the Winter Olympics

Fran Drescher: style icon and star of iconic 90s sitcom *The Nanny*

Gilmore Girls: the meaning of life

"Girls Just Wanna Have Fun": my jam

Godspell: my first musical (Hunter Parrish is a very sexy Jesus.)

Gordon Bombay: coach of The Mighty Ducks (Is it just me, or is Emilio Estevez circa 1992 a total babe?)

Hallmark Channel: a family-oriented television channel finally entering into the 21st century and embracing more diverse storylines (If we didn't already watch all 40 of their Christmas movies every single year, this would be a good reason to start.)

Hilary Duff: the iconic Disney Channel "it girl" and star of tween comedy series *Lizzie McGuire* ; essentially the Annette Funicello of the early 2000s (Oh wait, you don't know Annette Funicello? Looks like my glossary needs a glossary.)

Home on the Range: an often-fogotten 2004 Disn-aster

Hulk Hogan: father of incredibly successful actor, singer, and model Brooke Hogan

Hunting an Internet Killer: nightmares for weeks (Live in ignorant bliss, I beg of you.)

Ice Men: an all-male sychronized skating troupe of regulation hotties that performed for charity throughout the early 2000s

Jack Bauer: lead protagonist of the hit television series *24*; played by Canadian actor Kiefer Sutherland, also known as "that guy who takes off his pants when he gets too drunk at the bar"

Jaime Sale: radical anti-vaxxer and anti-masker who seems to have lost her marbles after divorcing delicious daddy David Pelletier

Jake Gyllenhaal: sexy but smelly

Jenga: a board game; used in a sentence, "No, I absolutely will not play Jenga with you."

Jiggly Caliente: trans fashion icon, despite her "more is more" mentality during the fourth season of *RuPaul's Drag Race*

Jinkx Monsoon: winner of the quintessential fifth season of *Rupaul's Drag Race* ; nerdy and narcoleptic, Monsoon is truly a winner "of the people for the people" (But apparently RuPaul can't even remember her name. Senior moment, much?)

Joe Goldberg: I liked him better on Gossip Girl

John Cena: a wrestling icon who gained major attention from "the gays" after stripping down to his underwear and dancing his rock-hard buns off in HBO's *Peacemaker*

Jonathan Van Ness: my dream skating partner

Judas: an electro house bop released by Lady Gaga in 2011

Judy Garland: a Hollywood legend best known for portraying Dorothy Gale in the cinematic masterpiece *The Wizard of Oz* and affectionately known as "Little Miss Show Business;" recorded a phenomenal trio of vocal jazz albums from 1956 to 1958 with arrangements from icons Gordon Jenkins and Nelson Riddle featuring signature songs "Come Rain or Come Shine" and "Zing! Went the Strings of My Heart" (also see "my favorite human")

Julia Roberts: robbed of the 1991 Best Actress Oscar

Kalteen Bars: Swedish nutrition bars designed for weight-loss; go ahead, give them a try

Kesha: I knew her when she was Ke$ha

Kristi Yamaguchi: 1992 Olympic Champion referenced in "Hotel Nacional," Gloria Estefan's underrated bop; "Going for gold like Yamaguchi / It's time for Hoochie Coochie"

Kylie Minogue: Kylie, my love. If you're reading this, we are all thirsty for another North American tour. Capital. T. Thirsty.

Lifetime Network: budget *Hallmark Channel*

Little Debbie: a line of snack-sized desserts produced and distributed by the *McKee Foods Corporation* (Would anyone be surprised to find out that these snacks are actually more plastic than food? Nope. Didn't think so.)

Macaulay Culkin: a child actor best known for his roles in the first two *Home Alone* films, as well as *My Girl* and *The Pagemaster*, struggled with a very public drug addiction throughout his adult years (But his 2020s glow-up is hella iconic).

Mackenzie Scott: generous philanthropist and ex-wife of the vastly inferior Jeff Bezos

Madonna: the OG "material girl"

Meryl Streep: gay god

My Favourite Human: Judy! Judy! Judy!

Nana Mouskari: legendary Greek singer known for recording hundreds of albums over the course of an almost seven-decade career; but, like, meh

NSYNC: an iconic boy band forced to disband after lead singer Justin Timberlake said "Bye, Bye, Bye"

Olivia Newton-John: there's a very good chance that Brad would have asked for a divorce if she didn't make the book

One Life To Live: a steaming pile of garbage

Paris is Burning: a 1990 documentary chronicling New York ballroom culture throughout the 1980s; provides an enlightening look into the horrific experiences of trans sex workers

Peggy Lee: best known for her 1958 rendition of "Fever" and her work on the soundtrack of Disney masterpiece *Lady and the Tramp*; a trailblazer for women in the recording industry

penny candy: a wide variety of sweet treats, including gummy bears and tootsie rolls, available at the 7-Eleven for one cent (Without the penny are they now called nickel candies? Or do you have to buy them in groups of five? I have so many questions. The world has changed, man.)

Pingu: a bizarre stop-motion children's series about a penguin with severe anger management issues

Piper Laurie: an American actress best known for portraying Margaret White in Stephen King's *Carrie*, a role for which she was nominated for an Academy Award for Best Supporting Actress

Pontiac Firebird: a very sexy car

Rachel McAdams: one time, Regina George rode right past me on her bicycle; it was awesome

Real Housewives, The: #goals

Rita Skeeter: a bitchy witch journalist known for spreading "fake news" in the *Daily Prophet* and antagonizing Harry Potter

Rocky Balboa: somethin' about fightin'

Sabrina the Teenage Witch: a 1996 sitcom starring Melissa Joan Hart as everyone's favourite adolescent enchantress; vastly superior to the 2018 Netflix series *Chilling Adventures of Sabrina*

Sally Field: won the Academy Award for Best Actress twice for her roles in *Norma Rae* and *Places in the Heart* (Sometimes when I became really angry with my own mother, I would tell her that I wished Sally Field was my mom instead.)

Sara freaking Bareilles: she's not gonna write you a love song

Scrooge McDuck: wealthy uncle of Donald; enjoys swimming in his vast piles of mulah

SEARS Wishbook: porn for beginners

Snow White and the Seven Dwarfs: the first fully-animated feature-length film and my very first *Disney On Ice* show

Spice Girls: Wait wait wait … you don't know the Spice Girls? Why are you even reading this?

Sony Discman: an incredibly inconvenient iPod

Toy Story 3: the saddest movie of all time

Untucked: the official *Rupaul's Drag Race* aftershow; a star-making vehicle for Shangela Laquifa Wadley ("I don't have a sugar daddy. I've never had a sugar daddy. If I wanted a sugar daddy, yes, I could probably go out and get one because I am what? Sickening!")

Valentino: an Italian luxury fashion house; like Versace, but classy

Virginia Woolf: a prolific English author and pioneer in the stream-of-consciousness writing style; suffered from severe mental illness throughout her adult life, which her family referred to as her "madness"

Wild, Wild West: one of the most expensive films ever made; swept the 20th Golden Raspberry Awards in 2000 (including the award for "Worst Original Song")

Working Girl: starring Melanie Griffith, Joan Cusack, Sigourney Weaver, and a sexier than ever Harrison Ford, how could we not claim this iconic feminist film as queer canon?

Windows 95: a game-changing Microsoft operating system; decimated the careers of an inestimable number of technologically-illiterate Boomers

You're Invited to Mary-Kate and Ashley's: a direct-to-video series featuring the Olsen twins and a slew of their closest on-screen friends, singing and dancing along to insufferable original songs at a variety of themed parties (Thanks to my sister, I've seen them all more times than I care to admit.)

zaddy: a "hot as fuck" dad

"Zero to Hero": the second best song from Disney's *Hercules*

About the Author

Joe Bainbridge was born and raised in the tiny town of Corunna, Ontario. He moved to Kitchener to pursue a career in teaching, and later Toronto to pursue the love of a good man. His real-life experiences as a queer pairs skater were the inspiration for this project. Alyssa Edwards is his favourite drag queen, and *Queer Musings of a One-Time Boy Skater* is his first book.

Printed in Great Britain
by Amazon

83169351R00113